The Care and Counseling
of Youth in the Church

Creative Pastoral Care and Counseling Series
Editor: Howard J. Clinebell
Associate Editor: Howard W. Stone

The Care and Counseling of Youth in the Church

Paul B. Irwin

Fortress Press   Philadelphia

"All real life is meeting."*

Martin Buber, *I and Thou*

Library of Congress Card Number 74-26334

ISBN 0-8006-0552-7
Fourth printing 1984

1459H84   Printed in the United States of America   1-552

To the memory of
B. W. AIKEN
Adult Guarantor
to
Countless Numbers of Youth

Contents

Series Foreword

Let me share with you some of the hopes that are in the minds of those of us who helped to develop this series—hopes that relate directly to you as the reader. It is our desire and expectation that these books will be of help to you in developing better working tools as a minister counselor. We hope that they will do this by encouraging your own creativity in developing more effective methods and programs for helping people live life more fully. It is our intention in this series to affirm the many things you have going for you as a minister in helping troubled persons—the many assets and resources from your religious heritage, your role as the leader of a congregation, and your unique relationship to individuals and families throughout the life cycle. We hope to help you reaffirm the *power of the pastoral* by the use of fresh models and methods in your ministry.

The aim of the series is not to be comprehensive with respect to topics but rather to bring innovative approaches to some major types of counseling. Although the books are practice-oriented, they also provide a solid foundation of theological and psychological insights. They are written primarily for ministers (and those preparing for the ministry) but we hope that they will also prove useful to other counselors who are interested in the crucial role of spiritual and value issues in all helping relationships. In addition we hope that the series will be useful in seminary courses, clergy support groups, continuing education workshops, and lay befriender training.

This is a period of rich new developments in counseling and psychotherapy. The time is ripe for a flowering of creative methods and insights in pastoral care and counseling.

Our expectation is that this series will stimulate grass roots creativity as innovative methods and programs come alive for you. Some of the major thrusts that will be discussed in this series include a new awareness of the unique contributions of the theologically trained counselor, the liberating power of the human potentials orientation, an appreciation of the pastoral care function of the ministering congregation, the importance of humanizing systems and institutions as well as close relationships, the importance of pastoral *care* (and not just counseling), the many opportunities for caring ministries throughout the life cycle, the deep changes in male-female relationships, and the new psychotherapies—such as gestalt therapy, transactional analysis, educative counseling, and crisis methods. Our hope is that this series will enhance your resources for your ministry to persons, by opening doorways to understanding of these creative thrusts in pastoral care and counseling.

Paul Irwin, the author of this volume, brings a rich background of life experiences to his task of focusing on ministry to youth. His professional dedication has been to experiential education—in the church and in the seminary. As a colleague for seventeen years at the School of Theology at Claremont, I have esteemed him as a caring, creative teacher. In his seminary teaching, in countless workshops for ministers, youth workers, and lay persons, and in courses at the church of which he is a member, he has demonstrated repeatedly his remarkable ability to communicate his deep confidence in the capacity of persons to grow. His genius as a teacher has been his capacity to relate—openly, warmly, affirmingly. One of our children, now a young adult, recalls fondly a stimulating church school learning unit Paul taught more than a dozen years ago.

Professor Irwin has been involved with youth and youth workers much of his professional life. "Children and youth," he declares, "have been my major interest as both pastor and educator." Through many summers spent as camp counselor to children and youth of varied backgrounds he has pioneered in interfaith and interracial camping. Recently retired from seminary teaching, he now serves as educational consultant, continually in dialogue with both youth and their adult leaders as workshop facilitator and instructor. In this book, the distilled insights of the author's broad and rich experience are available. The book is written for both the minister and the lay youth worker. This fact emphasizes the author's conviction that the pastor should be directly involved in working with youth, as part of a minister–lay worker team. The goal of the author, and of this volume, is to help youth "make it" on their "journey into maturity."

HOWARD J. CLINEBELL

Preface

The pastoral care of youth is normally listed high among the priorities of the church's mission to persons. Providing such a ministry, however, remains for many churches a major leadership problem. In *Profiles of Church Youth,* a study of Lutheran young people and their adult leaders, Merton Strommen finds that most pastors and lay leaders tend to exhort and to give information, feeling less competent to minister to youth in any more intimate and personal manner.* Among his corrective recommendations to the churches, Strommen calls for awareness of the whole person and a total approach to youth ministry that makes the good news of Jesus Christ more relevant to their personal growth needs. It is this nurturing approach to the whole person that I have undertaken to describe in this volume. I have chosen to call it *personal ministry.*

As I write these introductory words, I am reminded of Jesus' saying to Peter as evidence of his love of that disciple, "Feed my sheep" (John 21:17). I like to believe that it was concern for the individual, so consistently exemplified in Jesus' own ministry, that he had in mind when he thus instructed Peter. Personal ministry begins with this theological understanding of God's individualized concern and care; it also requires the insights and skills of the psychological and counseling disciplines.

Writing for both the professional and lay leader, I have focused upon typical leadership concerns and situations, illustrating them from actual experience. I am assuming that the guidelines here offered are relevant to the youth

*For this and all other notes in this book, see the Notes section beginning on p. 74.

ministry of all churches, small and large. Leadership, of
course, is at its best when such general principles are applied
with innovative imagination in the light of one's particular
ministering situation. It is hoped, therefore, that the instances of care and counseling here reported will motivate
the reader to reflect upon his or her own leadership, with a
view to fresh experimentation and more effective facilitation
of growth and development in the lives of youth.

In these introductory remarks I wish to make acknowl-
edgment of my considerable indebtedness to those persons
who contributed directly to the writing of this counseling
primer, particularly the young adult ministers to youth whom
I once taught and who, through a happy consultative association, have deepened my understandings of ministry. These
include especially Betsy Baker, Charles Mabry, John Mahon,
Stanley Smith, Dwight Sullivan, and Mary Ann Swenson.
Dr. Francis McOlash, Protestant Chaplain at the Riverside
State Hospital, Costa Mesa, California, is another who
shared out of his wisdom as counselor to young people. All
are graduates of the School of Theology at Claremont, California and I frankly esteem them as "co-authors." In addition
I am grateful for the encouragement and guidance of the
editor and associate editor of this series, Howard J. Clinebell, Jr., Professor of Pastoral Counseling of the School of
Theology faculty, and his colleague Howard Stone, Execu-
tive Director of the Interfaith Counseling Service, Scotts-
dale, Arizona. In this supportive company I also include my
wife Georgenia, teacher and writer, who served as handy
home consultant.

The reader will note the name of B. W. Aiken to whose
memory I dedicate my writing. Affectionately known as
"BW," this remarkable man founded and directed for many
years a camp for children and youth on the upper shores of
the Chesapeake Bay, a service of the Coatesville, Pennsyl-
vania YMCA. It was under his tutelage that I acquired my
initial understanding and love of the young and the spiritual
foundations for personal ministry. In the pages to follow I

shall describe such a person as an Adult Guarantor. He was Adult Guarantor to me and to countless other youth.

Finally, I say a "thank you" to the young people about whom I have written in describing my personal ministry. Should any one of them come upon his or her own story in these pages, I trust it will be read with an appreciation, born out of their own growth struggles, of the help it can be to other youth.

PAUL B. IRWIN

1. Personal Ministry

Mary, age fifteen, was an unhappy girl. Life at home was intolerable. Nothing she said or did seemed ever to please her parents. Especially distressing was her mother's negative attitude toward her boyfriend. There was constant bickering between them over time away from home and late hours. Mary saw her mother as old-fashioned, out of touch with modern youth, "just an old witch." One night while I was working in my study, Mary appeared, obviously distraught, saying explosively, "I'm running away! I'm getting married—tonight!"

How would one ministering to youth—pastor, youth director, lay leader—relate to Mary under these circumstances? Consider the alternatives.

One might say, "Mary, you know very well that running away is a foolish thing to do. You're too young for marriage, and running away will only . . . . Mary, I'm not going to let you ruin your life. Now, listen to me . . . ." Mary, of course, would not have listened. She would have heard these words as no more than an echo of her scolding parent.

One could be more understanding and gentle in giving advice: "Look, Mary, I know you are unhappy, but running away and getting married isn't the answer to your problem. I think you know that. All teen-agers go through a period of conflict and rebellion at home. You've got to give yourself time to grow up." The counselor might elaborate upon this parental admonition, adding that Mary should return home and talk things over with her mother. How often she had done that—gone home, tried to reason, only to end the argument by fleeing to her room in angry frustration!

However well-intentioned, such an approach would not

1

have met Mary's need. A perceptive counselor would have immediately dismissed her talk of running away and marriage as no more than attention-getting. That, of course, was Mary's need at the moment—attention, but understanding attention. She was saying, "I'm hurting! Hear me! Understand me!"

What, then, could a counseling pastor or lay leader say and do that might presumably be helpful under these circumstances? Mary was standing before my desk, face flushed, tears beginning to flow. "Things are not going well at home, are they, Mary?" In effect I had already heard her say as much. At that, Mary slumped into a chair and began to cry. I pulled my chair to one side and waited for the sobs to cease. Finally, I said, "Things get tough at times. Would you like to talk to me about it?" She nodded and after a few moments of sniffling and daubing at her tears, Mary began her story, looking up now and then to see if I was listening. Occasionally I would reflect her feelings and ask a question for clarification—not much more than that. After about an hour, our talk seemed naturally to end. Mary sat pensively, seemingly released from hurt and anger, saying after a while that perhaps it was time to return home. I suggested that she might like to talk again. She agreed, thanked me, and left.

Why did Mary come to her pastor that night? Wouldn't a church youth naturally turn to the pastor for help? Whether one does is conditional. Youth are ambivalent toward adults during the teen years, and not all who need help feel free to seek it from an adult, even from one's own pastor. The need for guidance is there alright, but youth respond to the offer of ministry only when the pastor or lay person "comes across" as an Adult Guarantor.

The Adult Guarantor

The model of the leader as Adult Guarantor is offered by the distinguished psychoanalyst and historian Erik H. Erikson in his study of *Young Man Luther.** The reference there is to Father Staupitz, head of the Augustinian Order of which

Martin was a student. Father Staupitz was the one who stood by Luther to affirm and counsel him during his emotional and theological crisis.

Being a Guarantor assumes of the leader a warmth, authenticity, and healthy outlook on life, a spirit of optimism and confidence in the future, and requires of him or her a living with youth that inspires respect, trust, and communication. It is the leader as Guarantor, able to bridge the generation gap with discerning and affirming presence, who gives assurance to a youth and guarantees, as it were, that he or she can successfully cope with the business of growing up and can eventually "make it."* To be technically effective, the role calls also for a working knowledge of adolescent development—what's going on in young life—and skill in the art of care and counseling.

Such leaders normally have their nurtured beginnings during the years of their own adolescence and young adulthood. The exciting summers of my early life spent on the shores of the Chesapeake Bay as camper and leader unquestionably laid the foundations of my personal ministry. There I learned to understand and to love the young. When one has engaged in extended experiences of sports and campfire activities, leading devotional services and discussion, telling stories, walking the homesick child, and nurturing the fellowship of a cabin group—familiar experiences to many a youth leader—the beginning pastor and lay person have ready entry into the church's youth peer culture. It was supervised clinical training and development of group facilitating skills during university and seminary years that completed my preparation for the pastoring role of minister to youth.

Mary had come to my study that night apparently having sensed something of the Adult Guarantor in her minister. A pedigree of formal training and past experience, however important, is not in itself inviting to the young. The opportunity to be helpful must be earned in the context of the peer culture at hand. Announcing one's availability—"I'll be glad to see anyone in my office"—is not persuasive to the troubled.

The trust that is required is learned within the fellowship. The leader as Guarantor must be a participant in the life of the group. It was the emerging sense of such community that opened the door for me to engage in personal ministry.

Learning the Role

The role of Adult Guarantor to youth in the church is one that *can* be learned. It can even be refined and developed right on the job. My formal training and informal experience were early combined—and tested—in the parish at the point of program planning intended to help young people understand themselves during this difficult adolescent period of growing up. Indeed, one series of lecture-discussions was expressly given the title "Understanding Ourselves and Others." The popular feature was the use of case studies from current guidance material.* These were mimeographed and distributed to all members of the Sunday evening fellowship. Teams of senior high and junior college people functioned as a panel, after which their diagnostic comments and prescriptive proposals were discussed in small groups. My role was that of panel moderator and group discussion facilitator.

One case presented fifteen-year-old Frank whose parents reported him to be disruptive at home and uncooperative at school. Information about the family included mention of the mother's busy church and community schedule, the father's absences due to business, and troubled sibling relationships. After the case had been read, these questions were put to the panel of older teen-agers: What do you think is happening to Frank? How is he feeling? What do you think is causing the problem? How do you feel about Frank? What do you think would help the situation?

Note that the first question does not read, What do you think is *wrong* with Frank?—a common way of looking at persons in trouble. Frank is indeed a troubled person, but his problem is within the range of the normal. Young people know this to be an "everyday" problem and are quick to suggest—often with insight—both cause and cure.

The purpose of the case method is to evoke ideas and feelings which can illumine problem situations faced by the group themselves. The adult leader's role must be exercised with care. Youth usually want to know how the leader stands on issues discussed, but at the same time they are impatient with any attempt to impose a position. The appropriate role is that of facilitating a growth experience by listening, picking up nonverbal communication, giving feedback, clarifying, and translating, keeping comments relevant, posing questions and proposing alternatives. The leader may break in: "I hear you, saying . . ." or "How do you feel about this way of looking at it?" Open-ended discussion encourages reflective testing of ideas and prevents the usually unproductive debate.

There were initially two kinds of responses to the case material used with our youth. One involved making comparison with someone known personally: "I have a friend who . . ." The leader must deal cautiously with "telling" of this kind lest discussion becomes a gossip session. A second response brought degrees of self-disclosure: "Yeah, I get put down like that at home!" Some shared quite personal experiences; others were probably content to pick up for private reflection clues to their growth problems. It is usually in the small group of five or six—or only two—that persons feel freer to talk out their own emotional concerns.

Not infrequently there was a third, sometimes belated, response. During and after the series a young person, dropping by my office to visit, would suddenly pause in the conversation and say, "You know what we were talking about the other evening? Well, I . . ." then he or she would begin to disclose some personal concern.

Mary had been a participant in one such "Understanding" series. I have no doubt that her coming to my office that night had been prompted by the discussion of those case studies and a feeling that she could trust a leader who had shared his insights into the problems and processes of growing up.

Personal ministry to youth begins with trusting relationship. It becomes effective as care and counseling when the leader, as Adult Guarantor, is able to look into the inner world of a youth with understanding of what it is like to live as an adolescent, what is really involved in growing into maturity.

2. Journey Into Maturity

While personal ministry to youth requires an understanding of adolescence through direct encounter with young people as individuals and as groups, a general working knowledge of the adolescent stage of human development enables the counselor–group leader to function with theoretical discipline. An illuminating interpretation in this connection is that provided by Erik H. Erikson in his deservedly famous book *Identity: Youth and Crisis.**

Adolescence is the experience of developmental transition or passage from childhood into life as an adult. Ancient myths dramatized it as a "hero journey." In its varied story forms the myth has the youth leave family and village, undergo trials and tribulation, slay a dragon or perform some other meritorious deed, and return home in triumph. Translated, adolescence involves leaving the sheltered and innocent life of childhood and entering into the precarious and demanding existence of personal decision and social responsibility. Erikson's interpretation of adolescence is, appropriately, journey-oriented.

If myth places adolescence in a dramatic frame of reference as journey, it is the psychotherapist's clinical practice and research that provide an understanding of its psychodynamic or inner-working character. As in myth, Erikson presupposes the journey to be goal-directed, a quest for "identity."

Some years ago, the psychologist Werner Wolff observed that all expressions of a preschool child's personality—spoken language, play, and relationships—are variations on a single theme, namely, the child's search for his or her self. All the child's behavior, he concluded, appears as an unconscious questioning of "Who am I?" and "What am I for?"* This behavioral questioning Erikson characterizes as "identity formation."

Identity Formation

Erikson believes that identity formation begins when the infant hears a name called by the nurturing family and responds with recognition. As the social environment widens, the growing person relates differentially to his or her community, identifying with those who affirm while trying to avoid those who offend. Parents, siblings, teachers, club leaders, and peers become the "significant others" from whom values and meanings are learned. It is especially the model adults with whom children identify, and from whom they appropriate their social roles and thus their social self. Indeed, a child is not one but many selves. There is, however, a silent ego process at work organizing and regulating these selves which with the onset of puberty functions to assimilate and/or repudiate them toward greater synthesis. Under normal, healthy, nurturing conditions this process continues through the period of adolescence until there emerges a unique configuration of role perception, attitudes, and behaviors along with what Erikson calls an accompanying sense of "self-identity."

Self-identity as the healthy fulfillment of adolescent development is a perception of psychological integrity or wholeness—an inner sameness and continuity—that is recognized and affirmed by the community of significant others. Subjectively, it is a sense of well-being and of worth to self and others. It is a state of matured existence that hears an inner voice say, "*This* is the real me," as William James expressed it on one occasion.† Concomitants of real "me-ness" are a sense of at-homeness in one's body, mastery over one's emotions, and "knowing where one is going." With the "completion" of identity formation the young person moves on toward adulthood with confidence and anticipation.

Erikson insists that the character and significance of any one stage, such as adolescence, cannot be fully comprehended apart from its integral relation to the whole life cycle. A summary of his "epigenetic principle" of growth, and of the self's negotiations with the environment during each of the early and later stages of development, is therefore important to include in this review of the Erikson model.

Stages of Development

According to Erikson's "epigenetic principle" human life develops according to a "ground plan" that regulates the passage of the person through a succession of interrelated stages from birth to old age. In each of the "eight stages of man" the self in its interaction with the environment is required to accomplish a task essential to healthy functioning. During each stage the person is confronted with a crisis with respect to this task. It is a developmental turning point experienced as both vulnerableness and strength. An existential decision must be made; one must accomplish the task and move forward toward the next stage or, failing, regress to an earlier level of adjustment. How well one copes with the crisis depends largely upon the outcome of previous encounters with the degree of challenge or threat involved in the new situation. Inasmuch as no one experiences ideal self-fulfillment, the struggle for healthy, authentic existence and the occasional need for special help is universal.

The first requirement of healthy selfhood is to experience, during the first weeks and months of natal existence, a *sense of basic trust,* a feeling of "inner goodness"—as a response to the love and care of the parenting ones—that emotionally assures the infant that life is trustworthy. When nurture is discontinuous (and it is inevitably so) the infant experiences insecurity and anxiety. A measure of distrust is essential to the safety of a child and to a mature and critical approach to life. Where there is a drastic loss of parenting, the person experiences acute "infantile depression" which, if unrelieved, leaves the child with a *sense of basic mistrust.* Maturing at this stage requires an appropriate balance between a sense of trust and a sense of mistrust.

As a basic sense of trust is learned in the months of infancy, there is established, according to Erikson, an ego strength that is especially needed during the crisis of adolescence. In this *virtue* lies the foundation of that life of faith which is required of the self as it undertakes throughout life to resolve the conflict between trusting and mistrusting, between the choices of good and evil. It is a faith nurtured by the world's great religions.

The second developmental task essential to healthy selfhood is achieving a *sense of autonomy.* This is an attitudinal response to toilet training within the boundaries set by parental authority. The crisis is learning self-control while exercising independence. Learning to "hold on" and to "let go" appropriately enables the child to affirm himself or herself with pride and esteem. The concomitant virtue is *free will* as the condition of growth toward discriminatory power and decision-making. During this period, between the second and third years, the healthy parent attitude toward the child is one of firmness moderated by gentleness. If the child loses out in the struggle of wills at this time, she or he experiences a *sense of doubt and shame* accompanied by feelings of smallness and powerlessness. When pressure requires submission and the crisis is resolved negatively, the child becomes apologetic, fearful of the future, and compulsive in behavior. Positive resolution prepares the way for youth's social participation with acceptance of "law and order."

Between three and five years, the age of *initiative,* a child becomes intrusive, bolting physically and mentally into the environment. Erikson describes this stage as "being on the make," expressed as insatiable curiosity, verbosity, happy competition, and conquest. It is a period of make-believe when social roles are imaginatively enacted in dramatic play. It is also the period during which conscience is formed. The problem for the five-year-old is to exercise initiative without becoming the object of over-protecting and restricting parents and teachers or of the rigid control of one's own sense of right and wrong. Unless there is positive resolution of this crisis, the child experiences a *sense of guilt* and views herself or himself as "bad." A stifled initiative converts the developing moral sense into vindictiveness. When the task is successfully accomplished, the self develops a *sense of purpose.*

From about the age of six through prepuberty, a child becomes preoccupied with schooling. Normally there is delight in doing and making with others, finding one's particular interest and abilities, and developing work discipline. The resulting *sense of industry* brings recognition and a feeling of pride. Failing to achieve the virtue of competence at this time leaves one with feelings of self-estrangement and inferiority, a serious handicap on entering adolescence.

Like each of the preceding developmental tasks, finding the unique self in the years of adolescence has its time of crisis. How the crisis is met, as in previous stages, will depend upon the coping resources accumulated from past encounters and how one now looks upon the future. If growing up is perceived as opportunity for greater freedom and creative pursuits and the ego strengths are available, the crisis will be met with quiet confidence. If moving toward the requirements of adulthood are perceived as threatening, the crisis can be noisy and painful. Many young people experience ambivalence with alternating moods of confidence and doubt. When the crisis is aggravated by unusual circumstances such as illness, organic impairment, or extreme environmental pressure, the young person may find it difficult "to take hold of life," and hence live with a sense of *identity confusion* or the more extreme condition of negative *self-identity,* that is, seeing himself or herself as a "nobody" or "somebody bad." Thus emotionally handicapped, the adolescent copes with crisis defensively. He or she escapes from the normal demands of growing up by such manuevers as procrastinating, shirking responsibility, truanting, dropping out of school, giving up a job, staying out all night, using drugs, engaging in petty and serious crime, or in other ways "copping out" from the "hero journey." To aid youth in enduring the stress and strain of these years and to prevent acute crisis and crippling damage to the self, Erikson urges families and the community to grant a "psychological moratorium," that is, to accept adolescence as a time of experimentation with social roles, meanings, values, and life-styles before having to make the irreversible decisions required of adulthood. Such understanding also includes an awareness of delinquencies during this time as the youth's desperate search for social acceptance and a chance to develop fidelity.

According to the Erikson schedule, the crisis of identity formation is reached during late adolescence or early young adulthood. Its renewal, however, may occur in later life with situational changes such as migration, loss of employment, death of a loved one, divorce, or retirement. The search for a new self is for such persons a recapitulation of the threats to existence previously experienced during adolescence.

Beyond the years of youth there are three additional developmental stages in which healthy and creative existence requires successful coping with crisis. The first is young adulthood during which one is faced with the need for *intimacy*—to be perceptively in touch with oneself and able to enter deeply into interpersonal relations such as friendship, love, marriage, and sexual union; failure results in *distantiation* or isolation and estrangement. The mature years of adulthood are given to *generativity,* a primary concern for the next generation, with the generative adult functioning as parent or teacher or engaging in any form of altruism in the interest of an enriched community; the self's failure at this point in life leads to a sense of *stagnation* experienced as interpersonal impoverishment, boredom, and preoccupation with self-concern. Advancing creatively into late adulthood, one experiences *integrity*—an acceptance of life's journey as good, and an appreciative identification with personal virtues of love and dignity. The life of integrity extended into old age is expressed in *wisdom* articulated as wit, knowledgeableness, good judgment, and a measure of insight into the ultimate meaning of life. Without integrity, one lives out the years with a *sense of disgust and despair.*

Continuing Adjustment

It should be clear that the intended focus of this review of the Erikson thesis is upon identity and its formation. The total life cycle gives context to the dynamic character of the formative process. Identity is never finally or fully "achieved" in the static sense. It has its beginning in infancy and remains subject to change and development throughout life until the powers of interaction with the environment wane.

In this regard Erikson comments upon the popularization of the life-cycle theory and the tendency to oversimplify his interpretation of psychosocial development. He would have us understand that the anxieties of infancy leave a residue of immaturity that remains throughout life and that, even under the most favorable nurturing conditions, coping with developmental crisis is never a complete victory for the struggling self. Persons "move up and down the scale of maturity," and what healthy existence requires are adjustments which strengthen the self so that one can live with a favorable balance of positive over negative movement.

With respect to youth, it is especially important for their leaders (and their parents) to know that an adjustment of unfavorable balance or apparent failure to cope healthily with a developmental task does not preclude a more favorable balance at a later period, assuming that the young person has access to and draws upon resources which give fresh perspective and emotional support to his or her quest for identity. It is the church's mission to provide such support through a personal ministry during the years of adolescence when persons seem peculiarly vulnerable to the vicissitudes of growing up.

Related to the importance of an understanding of the need for continued guidance is Erikson's eagerness to correct the overemphasis upon the conditioning role of parents. He is aware that pediatricians and psychiatrists tend to relate behavior problems and delinquencies almost exclusively to what parents did or did not do in the early years. But the total community is involved in the rearing of children. Television, for example, may well be a major factor in influencing the thought and emotional life of the young. The failure to take into account the multiple forces impinging on the process of growing up represents a false interpretation of human development and could mean the unjustified punishment of parents for the transgressions of their children and youth.

Making It Through Adolescence

At this point the reader may be asking what practical value the concept of identity formation has for the leader appreciative of the journey theory of adolescence. On one occasion I interviewed two young people in an effort to answer that very question. Erikson cautions that much of identity formation is an unconscious process discernible only to clinical observation. But there should be, I reasoned, ordinary behavioral signs which leaders can expect to find as they work with and reflect upon the life of their young people. Certain of these signs seemed clearly to emerge during my interviews.

The two young people, both juniors in high school, were members of a church youth group. After explaining the interview procedure to the assembled group I began the questioning by asking each interviewee in turn, "Who are You?" Now, Erikson warns that a verbal response to this question is not a wholly reliable index of a young person's progress toward successful identity formation. Interview data of this kind, however, does offer clues to a person's self-perception, that is, how the person sees and feels about himself or herself, and that is a datum of self-identity. The initial answers were the obvious ones having to do with name, address, and school. Directing my questions first to the girl, I then began to probe for interests, attitudes, and feelings.

Marilyn, an intellectually brilliant youth of seventeen, responded by wondering if one could ever really know oneself. "We keep changing from one stage and from one situation to another. But we are individuals with our own interests, particular ways of looking at life and living it." She proceeded to identify herself according to race, religion, socioeconomic class, and education. She spoke appreciatively of her Jewish background and acknowledged that it had greatly influenced her attitudes and life-style. At one time she had been sensitive about her Jewish minority status in the community but believed she had overcome feelings of discrimination because of peer acceptance. She made a point of being an accepted member of a Christian youth fellowship.

Marilyn talked enthusiastically about her schooling. She was a straight-A student. History and social studies had helped to give her an appreciative understanding of peoples and their differences. She spoke compassionately of the needs of "Third World" people and expressed the desire vocationally or avocationally to be of help to the oppressed. I asked her if she could name a historical figure whom she admired. She promptly named Benjamin Disraeli. She had carefully researched this British statesman and now spoke of him with detailed accuracy. She felt he had been a major influence in her projecting a career in government.

I was impressed with Marilyn's thoughtful and articulate response to my questioning and concluded that she was reaching a happy climax to her identity formation. She was in touch with her feelings, secure in her relationships, socially sensitive, historically oriented, and aware of direction for her life. There was a self-affirmation and feeling of "good me-ness" that was convincing. I felt confirmed in these value judgments when the school authorities announced a short time later that Marilyn's scholastic record would permit her to enter the university directly following her junior year. The school's diploma was to be awarded at the completion of her freshman year.

By contrast, Carl floundered through most of my interview with him. There were long pauses and words came haltingly throughout our conversation. In response to my questions about vocation Carl thought he might be interested in the pastoral ministry, but he gave only superficial reasons for this possible choice. His preoccupation during the interview was his membership in the church group, but here again his comments did not reflect assurance or security. Aware that he had been ill at ease during the evening, I invited him to visit with me in my office.

Carl appeared the following afternoon. After a few pleasantries, I began to question him about Sunday evening's experience:

"Carl, how did you feel about last night—the interview?"

"Oh, a little nervous, I guess. It's difficult to talk in front of a group like that."

"I'm sure it is, Carl. I want you to know I appreciated your volunteering. Can you say why you did volunteer?"

"I don't know. You said talking about yourself is a good thing to do or something like that. I thought it might be helpful."

"Helpful?"

"Well, my high school adviser says that I ought to start thinking about what I want to do after school."

"You mean thinking about a vocation?"

"Yeah."

"Last night you spoke of your interest in the church ministry."

"Well, to be honest, I really hadn't thought much about it. I like our minister and I guess that's why I mentioned it."

"Would you be interested in talking with him about the ministry? I'm sure he would be pleased to discuss it with you."

"Well, no, I guess not. I don't think I could be a minister."

"How do you mean?"

"Well, you have to be able to preach and things like that. That would be too much for me."

Carl and I talked further—more about his church group, vocational interests, family, and school. I learned later that while he talked eagerly about being a member of the youth fellowship, his participation was really only occasional. In our conversation he continued to refer to "them" rather than to "us." I also learned that Carl was intellectually abler than his passing grades indicated. He had confessed that he did not like to study, preferring to watch television and just "goof off." What little thought he had given to his future had been at the school adviser's prodding. I spoke to the adviser of my concern for Carl and learned that the school personnel regarded him as poorly motivated, confused, and in need of counseling.

Crisis in adolescence is the self's inner conflict between two developmental choices: movement away from childhood toward adult life or backward toward earlier levels of adjustment. Marilyn had chosen the journey forward and had found the satisfactions of personal affirmation and social approval; Carl was ambivalent and had yet to choose his direction.

Four Crucial Needs

What does it take for the Marilyns and Carls—for all youth—to "make it" through the identity crisis? What need–experiences reinforce the self's will to grow and to cope positively with the task of identity formation? Within the context of the Erikson view of adolescence, four needs are considered to be crucial: (1) finding acceptance within community, (2) deepening interpersonal communication, (3) shaping an ideology or vision of life, and (4) achieving vocational direction. All four have a vital importance for identity formation:

Selfhood is an emergent of the process of socialization and requires, in the first place, the continuous nurture of community for its identity and for healthy, creative existence. Youth must sense the acceptance and affirmation of their significant others—peers and model adults. A fundamental need is to find identification with a circle of friends and to live in relation to one's group with passionate commitment and fidelity.

Interpersonal communication during adolescence involves the growing person in increasing degrees of intimacy. This is a time of social experimentation—developing friendships, dating, falling in love, and preparing for marriage. To experience intimacy, Erikson tells us, one must have at least a firm sense of identity in the making, for intimacy requires a fusing of the self with another without fear of personal loss. For this reason, it is significant to add, many teen marriages fail. They are usually contracted as an unconscious means of finding one's identity and are thus more likely to cause the conflict of confused persons than to issue in the intimacy required for successful mating.

Failing to find one's place in community, in one's peer group, and unable to enter deeply into relationships with the beginning of young adulthood, a person becomes alienated, confused, and uncertain of his or her worth. Others are perceived as dangerous to one's well-being and social participation is conditioned by moods of hostility and aggression.

The task of formulating an ideology or philosophy of life begins when, with intellectual maturing, youth are confronted by life's meaning and purpose. The function of ideology is to give meaning to the vague inner states of selfhood, to bring order out of the multiplicity of historical events, and to offer a compelling vision of what life can be. It connects the past with the present and projects an image of future existence. It contains an idealism and a hope not only for one's own fulfillment but for the promise of a new society as well. It is in shaping a vision of life that youth begin to identify with the forces of history that have intersected with their personal experience and to find solidarity with their community and all of humanity. This enables them, despite the contradictions of values systems, to make commitment to society's cultural conservation and its evolutionary development. They thus move toward adulthood with a sense of devotion and fidelity. Failure to shape such a vision of life leaves youth without direction and subject to whim and chance.

The fourth need to be met is vocational orientation and decision. Indeed, ideology and vocation, an attitude as well as occupation, are mutually integral to that process whereby the young perceive themselves to be accepted and affirmed by society. To make a vocational commitment is undoubtedly one of the most difficult decisions for youth; they tend to become anxious in a success-oriented culture and hesitate to choose for fear that the choice may turn out to be other than the right one—the "successful" one—for them. Erikson voices the additional concern that democracy nurtures its youth in the idealism of self-realization through initiative and independence but makes it difficult for them to adjust to conditions of social and economic disruption. This is particularly true in times of depression, inflation, war, and its aftermath.

These four needs, so vital to identity formation, will be treated more fully in the chapters which follow. They constitute distinctive features of a youth ministry that takes seriously the implications of a knowledge of the adolescent journey. Due to the highly technical nature of vocational guidance, however, requiring as it does such specialized resources as testing materials and detailed information about schools and job opportunities, this need-area will be treated only in more general terms when we refer below—in chapter 4—to the McNassor model of identity counseling.

Journey and Pilgrimage

Erikson's theory of identity development with its rich insights for ministry to youth, may well be associated, as we have seen, with the image of a "hero journey." From a Christian perspective, however, the image itself may be of questionable use. Interpreting the life cycle in his book on *The Struggle of the Soul,** Lewis J. Sherrill, Christian theologian and educator, regards the journey or saga as a limiting image. He reminds us that, interpreted biblically, life is a "pilgrimage." The hero sings of human virtues, whereas the Christian pilgrim celebrates the gift of divine grace:

> Life as pilgrimage is open to more than the natural and human, so that human existence is consciously related not only to nature

and to humanity, but also to God who transcends nature and humanity.*

For Sherrill, pilgrimage is a more appropriate image than journey. On the other hand, from the point of view of pastoral care as the theoretical context within which personal ministry is described, the disciplines of psychology and theology represented by the two images are seen as complementary and both necessary to its rationale. Sherrill, the typically American, empirically oriented theologian, enthusiastically appropriates the data of theoretical and clinical psychology for the purpose of deepening our understanding of human behavior. Erikson, the psychoanalyst, in turn, observes that encountering the crises of life requires a faith nurtured by the world's great religions.

It is the dialogue between contemporary theology and psychology in our time that has given church leadership its most effective conceptual and practical tool for personal ministry. I am proposing, therefore, the juxtaposition of the two images—hero journey and pilgrimage—as the more complete perspective from which to understand adolescence in conceptualizing a ministry to youth. On the one hand, there are human qualities associated with the hero image, such as courage and risk, which are essential to successful coping with the identity crisis. On the other hand, it is the pilgrim who knows that these are the fruits of faith.

As I develop in the remaining chapters the crucial features for a ministry of care and counseling of youth in the church, I do so with this inclusive image–understanding of identity formation during the period of adolescence. I hasten to add that we who lead youth dare not assume of this generation that they will happily accept and apply either image to themselves. Youth are finding their own images. The two here proposed are offered for conceptual purposes only as we try to understand and grasp the significance of our task.

3. Youth Culture as Covenant-Caring Community

At the close of the program, the student minister drove several of the young people to their homes. Visiting with his last passenger, a new member of the group, he casually asked how she felt about the Sunday evening fellowship. When she answered hesitantly, he began to probe. Finally, she confessed that she didn't find the kids very friendly. The next morning the minister learned that she had probably come because a member of the congregation had become interested in her and had encouraged her to participate in the church's youth program: "She needs the association of your fine young people." That week the youth fellowship officers met for a planning session. Before business-as-usual began, the minister asked how they felt things were going. Surprised, they answered positively but wanted to know why he had asked. Resistant to thinking of their group as "clique-ish," they defensively agreed to test this perception through role playing. It was not until they had observed one player experience the feeling of rejection that they were able to take a second look at the quality of their group life.

The Peer Culture

Normally a youth wants passionately to belong to an accepting peer group. It is in the intimate peer group, the social structure of the youth subculture, that much of youth's search for self-identity occurs. As a partial substitute for the biological family with which the young person is now in developmental conflict, the peer group offers escape from irritating parental controls, grants rights and privileges of accepted membership, lends a feeling of at-homeness, gives social status, and, by dictating fads in dress, hair-styling, dating practices, and other leisure-time pursuits, provides norms which solidify youth's place in a world of precarious adolescent existence. It is the accepting social setting in which the young can experiment—as Erikson sees their need—before making the irreversible role commitments required later of members of the adult world. Peer group culture is indispensable and can prove nurturing.

Culture, simply defined by the anthropologist, is the way a corporate unit of people desire, feel, think, believe, and conduct their individual and collective existence. Each culture has a distinctive quality, an ethos or perspective and feeling tone, that binds people together, nurtures and sustains them, engenders commitment, and gives meaning and purpose to life. Ross Snyder, writing in *Young People and Their Culture,* observes that much of today's peer culture leaves youth with "a sense of grayness, emptiness, meaninglessness, confusion, and despair."* He urges the church's adult leadership to join with their youth in creating a culture that makes it possible "for each person to grow a rich and resolute inwardness," an inwardness that enables one to be self-directing and creative rather than "inward sawdust." There is a deep hunger for this kind of life, says Snyder, and the church must be about the business of bringing it into existence.

The culture concept of ministry finds corroboration in a theory of education that takes account of the dynamic and holistic character of learning. That is to say, educational procedure is not confined to traditional classroom instruction with its focus upon the acquisition of knowledge, important as this function remains, but engages the total self in a total environment. Learning to become a fully functioning, self-affirming, effective, and decisive person means to be involved in multiple creative experiences and a participant in a culture. For the church, that culture is best described as a covenant–caring community. Ministry is the facilitating of such a community.

The Youth Fellowship

A youth fellowship sponsored by the church is in terms of its very sponsorship and existence a caring community. In its beginnings, however, it is that only by formal definition, not experientially, for caring means an evolving concern for one another. Time and leadership can help bring the caring into being. Realistically, a church's youth fellowship is founded upon the gregariousness of youth and their need for a supportive peer culture. They come together mainly to see one another, to rap, engage in group activities, relate, date, and enter into friendships and in-and-out romances. Adult leadership will stumble in their religious ministry if this sociological need is not recognized, accepted, and educationally exploited. However, the togetherness which young people enjoy is not yet Christian group culture until there emerges a sense of identity as a People of God. The New Testament community or *ekklesia* (meaning to be called out or to be assembled) existed for the purpose of becoming a new humanity. It was to experience the presence of God in a fellowship of "two or three gathered together" in Christ's name that made them *the* caring community of the Greco-Roman world. The philosopher Tertullian observing these people remarked: "See how they love one another!" Because of their insecurity and anxiety about growing up, youth can be egocentric, jealous, competitive, prejudiced, hostile, spiteful, and out of sorts with themselves and their world. It is not until they encounter the living God through the love of Jesus Christ in a caring relationship that their togetherness unifies them as the koinonia of the first century, a fellowship of the Spirit. The gathered people become a Spirit fellowship when through continuing encounters of judgment and grace members sense the divine in their midst, undergo experiences of "dying and rebirth," and celebrate the new life in Christ.

Christian culture also requires the covenantal dimension of community. Members bind themselves with fidelity to one another and to the Eternal One in whose ultimate care they are nurtured and sustained on life's pilgrimage. Erikson's "moratorium," a time of experimentation, does not give random license to any behavior. Indeed, identity formation requires a certain integrity of performance; experimentation must be reasonably within the bounds of a moral and spiritual inheritance. This is not to discount the gains of the cultural revolution of our time with its new freedom and options for style. But with the advantages of cultural change come confusion, if not absence, of values and uncertainty as to life's meaning. Thus, a ministry to youth functions to call them to a covenant community—to the intentional, disciplined life in Christ. And this is the leader's challenge—to facilitate the creation of the covenant–caring community among the church's youth.

"Meaningful Space"

Ministry is where the people are. The perennial place for youth gatherings after school is the small upholstered booth saturated by background music from a juke box. It affords an intimate setting for that all-important rap session. While youth want this to be their own "thing," the *en rapport* adult leader can now and then drop in to say "hi" and to accept an invitation to jóin in the discussion. Somehow the situation and circumstances seem conducive to a greater feeling of freedom. People can raise questions, share experiences, and state positions. Community emerges easily from such encounters. A burger and coke locale can foster ministry as well as a church office. In both places the great issues of growing up in the world can be discussed if not settled.

If the church is to help create a peer culture, it can even provide such a locale, a youth center where the fellowship members can exercise ownership. The center, of course, must meet youth's own criteria of attractiveness and comfort. Such a center is usually clashingly colorful—walls lined with blow-ups, collages, graffiti, bulletin board notices, cartoons, chalkboard art, and "borrowed" traffic signs. Adult leaders sometimes need to convince the church fathers and mothers that do-it-yourself decor is essential to peer culture at-homeness.

These same supportive adults also find it important to provide their own residence as a second home for youth. Leaders learn that an "open door" policy is crucial to a ministry of care and counseling. A leader's home is a place to go when one has experienced "hurt self-identity," when things at home are not going well, when one is in serious trouble, or when one wants just to "hang-loose" and rap.

The pastor's office, the church center, and the leader's home are more than meeting places. As the existentialists would say, they become "meaningful space." There, all kinds of encounters occur; there, the self may experience that "rich and resolute inwardness" required of growth toward authentic self-identity.

Parental Support

Ministry, on the other hand, is not confined to a given place. Interests, projects, and adventures spread out in all directions into the larger life of the church and the environing community. Youth ministry at times becomes intergenerational, ecumenical, and global.

Ministry, as I have said, is where the people are. Knowing this, the minister will frequently leave his church office to visit in the neighborhood. In my parish that meant formal visiting in homes, but also just wandering about after school hours to meet the kids and be with them in their play. Actually participating in their sports and games is not essential to successful leadership with youth, but seeing fun in their leisure activity and sharing the fun with them does contribute to a confidence of relationship. It is a kind of caring. Being what the kids call a "good guy," however, does not make one a peer, nor should it. Out of their affection for a leader youth will often speak of him or her as a friend, even use the person's given name or nickname, but what they need and want in their leader is a maturity that precludes being "just one of the gang."

Visiting in the neighborhood opens opportunities not only

to be and share with the children and young people but also to become better acquainted with their parents. Even where a basic rapport exists between democratic parents and their adolescent children, there are still clashes over attitudes and life-styles. Parents tend to suffer from cultural lag and are often regarded by their youth as "old-fashioned." Parents tend to criticize the teen culture as something of a "disease" that infects the whole of society with what they consider to be immature goals in music, art, and literature. Youth's response to this charge is often verbalized in terms of adult "hang-ups."

Mature leaders exercise caution in their rap sessions and counseling lest in their support of youth's need for emancipation they overwean them from their parents. There must be support for the teen-ager who struggles against insensitive parental control; but it is necessary to recognize that for normal adolescents their basic source of growing-up security is in the parental relationship. Talking and working with parents, then, becomes an important aspect of one's ministry. It means, on the one hand, maintaining a confidentiality of relationship with youth, and, on the other, sharing with parents insights into the peer culture and providing parent enrichment–guidance opportunities including the growth group experience. Today the experimental intergenerational church school is with us attracting all ages from children through the grandparent generation in an exciting common learning-celebrating event. And the family night has been reinstated, with planning done not by an official committee but by members—including the children—of one or more families. There is evidence that children and youth, to say nothing of their parents, tend to thrive psychologically in a family support cluster composed of four of five compatible families who live with an interpersonal intimacy expressed in casual visiting and sometimes in planned activities including times for "talking over" the normal problems of everyday existence. The church can encourage, even sponsor such clusters—the extended family model—and offer resources such as the Thomas

Gordon program of Parent Effectiveness Training and intergenerational rap sessions.* But this caution: youth must be
left free to develop their own peer culture while the adult
support group remains in the background.

I have often asked parents: "What do you want for your
young people? How can the church help?" The responses
were of two kinds: "That's why we employed you—to tell us";
and, "Well, no one ever asked us before; let's see now . . ."
It was out of such conversations that neighborhood groups of
parents were formed to discuss youth, family life, and the
church's ministry in this regard. In time, from these informal
gatherings, there developed a highly motivated and cooperative support group of parents for our efforts to create a covenant–caring youth fellowship.

Some leaders complain that parents are reluctant to help
create the desired culture. There is a sincere desire expressed
by some parents that youth be given complete freedom from
parental influence in developing their group life. Others see
the importance of helping while keeping in the background;
they may chauffeur when asked, assist with "food" on occasion, open their home or patio for a special meeting, and
participate in intergenerational discussions. Parents are not
likely to contribute in these ways, however, unless they have
been cultivated to become such a support group.

Group Organization

How does a youth fellowship structure its corporate life to
help it function effectively in meeting the needs of its members? Often the constituency of the church is drawn from
widely separated areas of a community. How, for example,
does a downtown church nurture intimate peer relations and
a sense of total covenant–community among people from
outlying areas?

A common pattern is to organize according to the several
functions of a fellowship's core meeting, namely the Sunday
evening program. My experience has been to work with four
small groups which will plan and direct the feature events of

a given meeting: recreational fellowship, food, forum, and worship. The intent is to keep the groups small enough to foster interpersonal relating and to give each member opportunity to exercise leadership responsibility. Each group contributes to the life of the whole. Groups maintain their functional identity for one or two months, then accept a new assignment. At half year, group membership is rearranged. In addition, there are separate task forces working on such special projects as the newsletter or a social event, spiritual retreat, or conference. However, there are no hard and fast relational boundaries maintained, so that intermingling is enjoyed throughout the evening. Such freedom within structure fosters both the small group relationship and a sense of inclusive community.

The model, with variations, is a common one, but not all youth appear willing to accept and work within structure of this kind. Youth often complain of the pressure of the school week; they frequently prefer a more relaxed and open social atmosphere. Some leaders believe the need is justified and take a laissez faire attitude. Others feel that covenant— community is thereby lost and creativity sacrificed, but they find it difficult to facilitate change.

Democratic Procedure

There is no ready formula guaranteed to solve the problems of group life and organization. Democratic procedure, however, holds the greatest promise if applied with patience and insight into the dynamics of the peer culture. Jim's experience with democratic leadership, however, was rather different from that of Peter and Phyllis.

Jim learned democratic procedure the hard way. Only recently employed as a student leader, he began his story by confessing to frustration:

> For more than a month I tried to persuade them to settle down to a more serious type of Sunday evening program. I guess I had

been pressuring them. Finally, after doing some reading and reflecting I decided upon another tactic.

Jim invited the youth president to his office to talk things
over. His conversation with Karen was productive. At her
suggestion a second meeting was called at which the four
other officers were also present. Jim went on:

> I listened while they told me that the kids liked the Sunday eve-
> ning just as it was—eating, playing volleyball, and time just to
> talk and "goof off."

At that point Jim made the proposal he had shared with
Karen earlier. Sunday evening would remain a social time.
In addition, however, he would offer three group activities
for weekday participation. Attendance would be optional, of
course, but membership would be by contract only. A contract committed a person to attend at least the first four sessions of the eight-week schedule. Groups were to be limited
to eight to ten persons. Jim continued with his story:

> I proposed these three group activities: (1) a problem-centered
> "growth group," (2) a group to discuss the life-style content of
> selected folk music, and, (3) a study-discussion group on "Jesus:
> Hippie, Superstar, or What?"

After clarification, the proposal was accepted by the officers
as an experiment. "They agreed to go along with it on a trial
basis." The following Sunday the president made the announcement, called for discussion, and then for a vote. Within
a week the first two of the discussion groups were consti-
tuted with a combined total of nineteen contracts out of a
total membership of twenty-seven young people.

Jim was pleased at the new development, at his seeming
ability, after initial failure, to become a change agent. Two
factors seem to have been at work initially. In the first place,
he had inherited a "do-as-you-like" approach from two adult
leaders who worked in a friendly fashion with youth but

lacked training. Jim had been employed to replace them. In the second place, though trained, he was new on the job. He had tried to make changes before he had had time to establish the trust relationship—especially with his youth leaders—that is so essential to adult leadership. The fellowship officers defensively insisted that they were quite capable of directing their own program. The result was a stalemate in leadership and the absence of creative activity.

Then it was that the dynamics of the situation began to change. Confronted by a troubling problem, Jim began to read a book he had purchased some time before that was still unopened and gathering dust on his desk: *Games People Play,* a popular exposition of Transactional Analysis by Eric Berne.* Having read a recent review of it, Jim now dug into it, hoping to find out what kind of "games" his young people were playing.

> In no time "the lights went on" about my game-playing. I should have known that I had fallen into the "parent trap." I had been "transacting" with these young people out of my inner role as Critical Parent, as Berne identifies such behavior. I was scolding them and they were reacting like the resentful inner Child.

With his new self-image as discipline, that is, acting as the Nurturing Adult, Jim rose to the challenge of Berne's interpretation of interpersonal transaction and decided to exercise his leadership power in a more creative way.

His approach was to initiate a fresh relationship by inviting President Karen to his office—not to "tell" but to talk things over. He believed that in a relaxed atmosphere he could come across as an understanding person. He also assumed that if he listened he would get a hearing in return. His Berne hunches proved correct. There in his office the young president responded in a mature way—the Adult within the youth. Jim's warmth and openness was such that Karen could be honest about her leadership, acknowledging that she had capitulated to the wishes of the group for fear of losing status and acceptance among her peers. Her guilt feelings were relieved when she heard the student leader's proposal of compromise. Her co-officers responded with equal willingness to try change. The following Sunday evening Jim remained in the background, granting Karen the right to exercise her leadership with a new sense of confidence in the role. Jim enjoyed his new Adult self-identity and rejoiced at Karen's success. The favorable vote opened the way for a cooperative relationship between them to build a more creative and Christian fellowship.

Peter and Phyllis gained respect for democratic leadership a bit differently. The young married pair had brought their high school youth together for a night of "fun and games" to begin a weekend mountain retreat. Following "lights out" that first night an unofficial party got underway in one of the cabins to which an invited nonmember of the church brought several bottles of wine. After several rounds of drinks, a number of the revelers paraded noisily through the camp for hours, making loud and crude remarks.

Having been kept awake half the night, it was a bedraggled group of youth who assembled the next morning at the request of their adult leaders. Despite the early hour and the angry mood of some, Peter and Phyllis approached their task without getting "hooked" by the Scolding Parent attitude. They called for honest expression of feeling about the party and its aftermath.

Answers indicated the group's ambivalence: "It's all right to have parties after lights out; it's part of the weekend fun." "Only if everyone's invited." "How about being loud-mouthed!" "Is it all right to drink?" The pros and cons were expressed and explored, but it was the questioning concerning the nature and purpose of the retreat that apparently proved threatening and called forth the most heated remarks.

In such a situation leaders are faced with a delicate issue. Many young people, often including those deeply involved in the life of the church, look upon the institution as restrictive. They see the church as "always putting you down."

This group had the further problem of the presence of the

nonmember. Though initially responsible for the drinking, he said nothing during the discussion; nor were any remarks directed toward him. But his being there made discussion awkward. Later he approached one of the leaders to offer apology by saying that he had never before been with a church group and wasn't aware that there might be any question about drinking.

With breakfast announced, Peter and Phyllis terminated the discussion. At least the situation had been emotionally aired and rapport at the tables indicated a restoration of community. The retreat continued as planned without further incident. During the Sunday morning worship, a litany of confession and prayers for forgiveness and guidance were included in the order of service. Back home the following Sunday evening, the group reviewed and evaluated their experience. They concluded by agreeing to devote the next few meetings to a search of Scripture for an understanding of what it means to be a Christian youth group and to spell it out as a guide to their own fellowship.

Effective Adult Leadership

The experiences of Jim, Peter, and Phyllis clearly demonstrate two essential qualities of effective adult leadership among youth. All three leaders were personally mature and procedurally perceptive in coping with their respective crises. Jim was able to accept his faulty beginning as a youth minister and then to translate book knowledge into practice. Peter and Phyllis learned what happens when the leader finds an uncooperative individual in the group who needs special care and counseling—someone who can perhaps *learn by living* with other youth who in general respond appreciatively to understanding, affirming personal relations and open, democratic processes. Peter and Phyllis were mature in "keeping their cool" at a time of tension and division within their group and allowing for honest expression of aroused feeling. Equally important was their ability to use the occasion and appropriate the issue for the purpose of deepening the group's understanding of their own existence as a Christian community, a People of God. This is leadership at its best.

The first task of the church's adult leaders is to meet those conditions which nurture a climate of concerned and responsible participation among the youth themselves—to create the covenant–caring community. It is to encounter youth where they are and be discerning of their growing-up needs, but then to draw upon one's spiritual disciplines, apply democratic principles of procedure, and engage in experiences through which God in Christ becomes incarnate again in communication of the meaning and actuality of redemptive existence.

A second task, continuous with that of creating covenant–caring community, is to cultivate interpersonal relationship. Identity formation, as we have seen, requires the ability to relate to others with intimacy and significance. Leaders need to be aware of the importance of relationship, and there are processes that can prove helpful in achieving this end.

4. The Ministry of Interpersonal Communication

A young woman student and I met in the library one evening as we were checking out books. I inquired about an intriguingly titled paperback she held and was told that it was the story of the current charismatic movement. As we stopped to visit, Ann volunteered that she had dropped out of college for a year in search elsewhere of that elusive meaning to life, had returned for her senior year, and was now an enthusiastic member of an intentional, charismatic church group. As a result of her participation in Bible study, prayer, and speaking with tongues, she had "become a Christian." She was now planning a career in medicine as an expression of her commitment to mission. The paperback was a resource she intended using to interpret her recent conversion experience to meet a course assignment in religion. We were soon engrossed in conversation. For more than an hour we explored our respective pilgrimages, questioning and commenting until our mutual sharing drew us together as spiritual partners.

Adult-Youth Encounter

Reflecting later upon the encounter, I was reminded of Ross Snyder's concept of the Great Conversation, a conversation between an adult and a youth.* Such conversation is not formal counseling, not one person telling another, but communication between a caring adult and a searching young person that centers upon themes of deep existential significance for both. The Great Conversation may be an exploration of such themes as love and freedom; it may begin by reflecting upon the meaning of a book or movie; it may focus upon a disclosure of truth that has given one deepened self-understanding and a fresh sense of direction to life. It was the latter that had engaged my new friend Ann and me in conversation that night. Snyder reminds us that on such occasions the adults initially serve as midwives to the "birth-ing" of "rich and resolute inwardness," but in becoming an eventual partner in the conversation, the adults too are in-wardly enriched. Snyder adds that such conversation can occur in a group with one or more adults engaging the inter-ests and concerns of their young people.

Ruel Howe underscores the importance of adult-youth encounter for identity formation when he writes that in its absence youth tend to flee from life, either by neurotically turning within or by wasting their creative potential in out-ward aggression. He adds that in such instances it is this very "birthing" encounter that has the power to restore distressed youth to self-affirmation and healthy life-style.* One young pastor, who spends a portion of his week on a drug-infested high school campus, reports youth saying of his ministry of conversation that it is in the rap room that they "get their heads straightened out." Equally sought after for healing conversation is a retired California minister widely loved for his caring ministry; hardly a day goes by without youth, often in numbers, appearing at Allan Hunter's door seeking the opportunity to talk.

The ministry of interpersonal communication is universally indebted to the late Martin Buber's concept of the "dia-logue." For this Jewish philosopher-theologian, "All real life is meeting."† Buber's meeting or relating is of two primary categories: I-It and I-Thou. The I-It relation is an objective and instrumental attitude and approach to reality, an en-counter with the world of usable objects. In a technological society of tools and machines we are greatly dependent upon the I-It relation. Buber warns, however, that a preoccupation with the utilitarian stance toward life infuses a culture and its people with the spirit of materialism and manipulation. The danger is that we become lovers of things and users of persons, indeed, we ourselves become "thingified."

The relationship by which persons become truly human and committed to a humanistic use of things is the dialogic I-Thou relation. I-Thou relating is the experience of making oneself a presence to the other one, of "crossing over" with sensitive and appreciative awareness of life from that side. It involves a sensing of integrity and worth in the other, an experience of mutual understanding and of interpersonal enrichment. Buber's seminal insight is that when genuine dialogue occurs the lines of relationship extend until God is sensed as present and between the parties. In Buber's own words, the experience is a "glimpse through to the Eternal Thou."* Communication becomes communion.

Growth Group Experience

The ministry of interpersonal relating has also been influenced by the Human Potential Movement of our time. Appropriating the processes of group dynamics and psychotherapy, the movement offers an "intensive group experience" for purposes of emotional health and personal enrichment. Its importance and popularity is noted in an interpretation of responses to a recent questionnaire which presents a picture of today's sense of personal "lostness."† The researcher, a pastor, observes that as physical distances between people shrink in our urban society, interpersonal distances widen and there is increasing loneliness, anxiety, isolation, and fragmentation. No wonder, he adds, that people are turning to the group encounter centers, sensitivity labs, and communication workshops which have mushroomed across the nation.

The church, historically committed to group experience, has found helpful resources within the Human Potential Movement. Especially among youth the "growth group," as it is commonly called, has become a major means of helping them to cope with the identity crisis. The early history of one such group documents the typical functioning of growth groups, their content, and the role of the leader.

After an evaluation of the life of their youth fellowship, the adult-youth leadership team agreed to supplement Sunday night activity with a "growth group" experience. They explained purpose and procedure and provided contracts for group membership. A signed contract meant commitment to the initial four sessions and responsible participation. The announcement was repeated in the weekly newsletter with time and place indicated for a meeting of three groups numbering from eight to ten members each. Homes were volunteered to provide comfortable accommodations and privacy. Each group was to be led by a team of two leaders.

On the first night, Harold and Helen had the eight members of their group take places in a circle with the co-leaders themselves seated directly across from one another. Harold called for attention and requested the signed contracts. With these in hand he explained the purpose of the group, focusing upon here-and-now experience, honest disclosure of feelings, and confidentiality. He elaborated briefly and replied to questions. Helen then introduced a game in which each person named a favorite color and then shared the reason for his or her choice. A similar game followed, involving the choosing of an animal and explaining the meaning of one's animal identity. The experiences were then debriefed for emotional responses. The sharing had both humorous and serious content. The group was then asked to fantasize an exploration of the inner self and to share their "findings." Whether instructions were confusing or the exercise threatening, participation was minimally productive. Sensing the group's restlessness, Harold proposed "dyadic conversation." They were asked to choose a partner and then sit apart from the circle in pairs to share "an experience of joy and of sorrow from the past six months." Dialogue during this period was so rewarding that all protested when time was called.

Even though they knew one another as members of an existing peer group, the youth were initially ill at ease. The evening began with much chatter, milling about, fussing with seating arrangements, and nervous laughter. Expecting normal anxiety during this first experience, Helen and Harold had chosen games to create a relaxed social climate and to engage the members in interpersonal encounter in a non-threatening way. One growth group leader reports that his young people will seldom "open up" until trust has been established through the use of various nonverbal, action-type exercises. It was a discerning move by Harold quickly to introduce paired conversation when the fantasy exercise apparently proved threatening. Trust is essential to self-disclosure, and research indicates that trust is more readily experienced in the one-to-one encounter than in the larger group relationship.

The use of two leaders is not only mutually supportive, especially for beginning leaders, but the presence, as in this case, of both a man and woman also creates a surrogate setting conducive to family-like dynamics. Harold and Helen alternated in role responsibility according to plan but felt free to act spontaneously. They confessed to forgetting a final debriefing. Evaluation adds a dimension to the group's learning and offers data for future planning. It can enhance leadership effectiveness.

Feedback the following Sunday clearly indicated positive response to the growth group experience. Members liked especially the assigned topic for conversation. They requested the leaders in planning future sessions to assign a topic, with the understanding that other emerging interests might also be discussed. As it turned out at the next session, the assigned topic of "responsibility" was soon discarded when one member expressed concern about an impending divorce in her family. "Divorce" immediately became the theme. Carl Rogers, describing his leadership of encounter groups, accepts such sudden shifts of focus so long as they remain personally meaningful and involving for all. * The problem for Harold and Helen this time was to help several of the members discover the personal relevance of the topic. The tendency was to talk in generalities about divorce, whereas the accent in growth group discussion ought to remain the self-involving here-and-now experience.

Sexuality was the requested topic for the third meeting. Participation began with a "word association" exercise related to the terms "sexuality" and "sex," and this was followed by individuals sharing a fantasy relationship with a sexually attractive person. The fantasy sharing led to a free-wheeling discussion of the group's own relating and dating practices. With diminishing inhibition the boys began to engage in a competitive comparing of dating "conquests." The girls, reacting uncomfortably to this exchange, withdrew from participation. Leader comments intended to facilitate a healthier situation were regarded by the boys as judgmental, but had the effect of at least moving the group into a discussion of the social and ethical context of sexuality.

Helen and Harold were faced with a delicate problem during this third session. In a growth group freedom is needed if topics are not to be discussed superficially, and especially if, as in this case, sexuality is not to be treated prudishly. However, guidelines can help a group deal with such important and difficult matters as sex with a sense of propriety. A leader can say at the outset, "Let's talk openly and honestly about sex, but let's also be sensitive to feelings about a very personal matter. We should be especially careful that our remarks do not expose another person, whether present or not. We are here to share responsibly and to learn from one another what sex is about and how we can best express our sexual self." This sets reasonable boundaries for discussion. A wise youth leader of many years advises that it is not helpful and may likely be harmful to "throw back the covers completely."

Disciplined growth group leaders do not indulge in authoritative answer-giving, but facilitate reflective discussion and the sharing of feelings and attitudes. On the other hand, they are also obliged to function knowledgeably. Harold and Helen found it an important asset to have in hand biological, sociological, and ethical data bearing upon sexuality. It is equally important for leaders to know that young people, especially during the years of puberty, experience feelings of guilt about their emerging sex life which are not relieved by merely acquiring scientific facts. A major function of the growth group is to help members come to terms with their emotional life.

Harold and Helen felt that the fourth session of their growth group was both confrontive and redemptive. Early in the discussion, Ken volunteered that he had been thinking lately about God, wondering if there was a God. Before the group could launch into what promised to be a deeply involving issue, Liz challenged his reference to God as male deity. After the exchange of words had become emotionally charged, Helen broke in to move the encounter toward a more therapeutic expression of feeling. Ken acknowledged that he found it difficult to show his feelings. With this, Helen said to him, "Ken, tell Liz how you feel about her right now. Come on, tell her!" Ken remained immobile for moments, obviously struggling with himself. Then, staring at his adversary, he suddenly cried, "I hate you!" There was utter silence in the group. Ken just sat there looking painfully at Liz. After what seemed an interminable time, he then slowly left his place in the circle, walked over to Liz, stooped, and kissed her. Liz did not speak, but she did respond with full embrace. Having been released to express honest emotion, Ken was also freed to risk forgiveness and reconciliation. It was a moment of grace for the entire group.

Contributions of the Growth Group

What developmental needs are met in groups of this kind? What does the growth group contribute to the handling of self-identity crisis? Research done with psychologically immature persons at the Human Development Training Institute in San Diego, California is suggestive.* The researchers Bessell and Palomares observed, first, that these persons seemed not to be *aware* of their own thinking, feeling, and behaving; out of touch with the conflicts and drives within themselves, they had no understanding of their actions upon themselves and others. Second, these persons seemed to lack *mastery,* i.e., the ability to cope with the situation at hand. A typical reply was "I can't." Their expectation was to fail and usually they did. Third, they evidenced ineptness in *social interaction.* They appeared to lack understanding of what it takes to get along with others, to like and be liked, and to enjoy genuine friendships.

While the research was done in clinical settings with disadvantaged children and youth, the Institute personnel concluded that these three needs, *awareness, mastery,* and *social interaction,* are common to all persons. The researchers also believe that a program of growth groups is beneficial to normally maturing youngsters as well as to the emotionally handicapped. The Institute has trained more than 8,000 public school teachers across the nation who now use what they call the "magic circle" with children and the "circle session" for young people.

In his writing on "encounter groups," Carl Rogers describes what occurs psychologically in such groups over a period of time.* My own experience as leader-observer and participant-member bears out his observations. I have seen the following occur where the growth group process is in operation:

1. Leaders who have the ability to relate with warmth and acceptance create a psychological climate of security which reduces defensiveness and encourages freedom of dialogic communication.

2. In this climate, persons develop trust; they feel free to relate with openness and to express honest feelings about themselves and the other group members.

3. In this nonthreatening atmosphere one can accept feedback and thus learn about oneself from the dialogue.

4. With new self-understanding, members are enabled to examine their ideas, values, attitudes, and behavior; they can begin to experiment with change.

5. The individual not only perceives personal growth within but senses growth in the group as well; the peer group moves toward authentic community.

6. With new insights and affirmations of self, the person enters again into his or her world of everyday existence with a fresh sense of meaning, self-confidence, and directional satisfaction.

From a theological perspective, there is an additional value dimension to growth group experience. When the group's transactional relationship reaches the level of genuine "dialogue"—as Buber interprets I-Thou encounter—it can become for the participants an authentic religious experience. Thomas Oden, a theologian who has taken seriously the "encounter culture," sees in it a demythologized pietism with historical roots in such eighteenth-century renewal movements as the Jewish Hasidism (Buber's cultural-religious heritage) and Wesleyan evangelicalism.* The encounter culture and the earlier renewal movements are alike, he notes, in their stress upon here-and-now verbal encounter in the context of supportive interpersonal relations. Oden finds in the encounter group the secular equivalent of the Christian experience of redemption. When persons experience unconditional acceptance and love from their group neighbors, they are released from anxiety and guilt. In his critique of the secular encounter culture Oden points out that the trustworthiness of the saving group—the necessary condition for the experience of "death and rebirth"—is of an ultimate source made explicit in the Christian kerygma. Leadership, he adds, does not create trust; trust is of God. A group becomes distinctively Christian when it becomes aware of the transcendent character of shared experiences and lifts its response of thankfulness to the level of celebration and worship. For the Christian, it is within the caring community that the miracle of "salvation" (from the Latin term *salvus* meaning health) occurs.

Writing on behalf of youth, Oden confronts the adult leaders of the church with the loss of credibility unless they "nurture communities that embody love, forgiveness, and reconciliation," actualities for which words so easily become inadequate substitutes.* It is in the encounter or growth group as Oden describes it at its theological best that youth find a spirit–community in which they can work through their anxieties, find release from the soiling experiences of unhappy experimental life-style, gain fresh perspective on the pilgrimage, and "renew a right spirit" within.

"Identity Conversation"

Although the ministry of interpersonal communication should be continuous in the life of the church, there are particular times when planned relationships are peculiarly significant. I refer to developmental crises and periods of transition. Interpersonal ministry as conversation and group discussion have long been used effectively in relation to the *rites of passage.* During early adolescence, when youth have "come of age," pastors and associates in most churches meet with their young people to prepare them for the church's confirmation of their new status as full members of the congregation. During this time of identity crisis, however, a ministry of interpersonal relating should be equally important.

My recommendation for such an occasion would be an adaptation of the Donald McNassor rationale and model for high schools.† Educator McNassor has discovered in his research seminar in school counseling that students in their senior year react with anxiety as they approach the day of graduation. The seminar reports: "One is struck by the kind of tranquilized mood the students have created for themselves . . . they seem partially paralyzed for action such as talking with people, making inquiries and specific plans. They are waiting, waiting for what they call the big change to come."‡ The researchers conclude that when students begin to comprehend that they must soon "stand alone and find their real identities . . . behavior tends to become regressive."

Carl, you will remember, expressed this same anxiety

when asked if he looked forward to graduation. To meet an obvious counseling need at this time, McNassor has designed for high schools a program of "identity conversation." All twelfth-grade students are given opportunity by invitation to meet with members of the counseling staff to discuss "the perplexing questions asked by all youth today." Group meetings for such discussion are followed by optional visits for individual talk.

My proposal follows this pattern. I would have all pastors or the staff person most closely related to youth, invite those youth anticipating graduation from high school to visit with them for "identity conversation." The invitation, written and personally addressed, would be to meet first for group discussion and later, if desired, for individual conversation. I would recommend the issuing of invitations early in the fall term before final decisions and plans are made for the future or before the tranquilizing mood sets in. The purpose would be to assist and give perspective to decision making at this important juncture of life.

McNassor offers leaders a list of questions to stimulate discussion.* His list—supplemented with some additions intended to provoke specifically theological dialogue about concerns of personal faith—would be appropriate for the church's use:

As you look ahead to graduation, what do you think you will be doing next year? What tentative ideas do you have about this?

What are some hopes or thoughts you have as to what you want to be and do, as plans for the future? When did you decide this? Have you sought information and counsel about it?

If you have time and means some day, what would you most like to accomplish?

How does the world look to you today? Where do things seem to be going? How does this fit with the life you want to live and what you want to do?

Do you see anything in the world and the future that you

feel is worth being deeply concerned about, something that people ought to do something about?

Most people get down in the dumps occasionally. Has this happened to you? What was going on?

What three objectives best describe you to yourself?

McNassor reports enthusiastic response from students. I would expect the same response from church youth whose pastor has invited them to talk over these matters. On the Sunday when the graduates are named and congratulated from the pulpit, such recognition is likely to have deeper personal significance for everyone—pastor, youth, and parents alike.

In a day of continuing education and the flourishing of workshop training in methods of interpersonal communication and counseling, the church does well to invest leadership time in such opportunities. Youth will respond to these ministries which reach deep into the self and help them to grow "a rich and resolute inwardness," relate responsibly and redemptively to one another and to the world, and experience the Eternal Thou-ness in human existence.

5. The Ministry of Individual Counseling

The traditional concept of individual counseling has long connoted a clinical relationship between counselor and counselee occurring in a formal interview. The model to be described in these pages, however, is one of pastoral care. It includes the interview, of course, but extends counseling also into the various avenues of encounter within the larger community life of youth. That is to say, counseling with youth may occur under a variety of circumstances and in unconventional settings. Frequently, a youth will linger at the close of a meeting, ostensibly to help put things in order, and while working casually speak of some personal concern. Retreats and camping are conducive to confidential talk—on the trail, under the oak, at the beach, before the fire. Any place may become "meaningful space" for the counseling relationship to occur. If sustained counseling seems the appropriate next step, appointments can be made. The pastoral care model also calls for the use of community resources and the arranging of environment for therapeutic growth. It is consistent with the concept of creating a culture in which multiple experiences contribute to identity formation as pilgrimage.

A Pastoral Care Model
Richard was not a member of my church youth group, but this did not preclude the possibility of my having a counseling relationship with him. Richard was a boy who frequently invaded the family lives of his peers, stayed too long, and in general made a nuisance of himself. For some reason he never wanted to go home. After a phone call for help late one

night by a youth's frayed parent, I knew action had to be taken.

At my urging Richard had been invited to attend a Sunday evening youth meeting. As he walked into our center that night, the social climate changed abruptly. His reputed aggressiveness and bizarre behavior made him less than welcome. It was during our early recreation period, while several of us were throwing darts, that I greeted him and invited him to join the elimination contest. Richard not only talked a good game; in short order his cockiness and skill reduced the dart players to the two of us. I observed him—stocky build, dark unruly hair, acne-infected face and neck, exceedingly talkative, and a flashing smile with every bull's-eye. His vocabulary marked him as intelligent and well-read for one his age, and in a social setting such as this his verbal talent was undoubtedly used to gain attention. I guessed that Richard would "muscle" his way into any situation out of compulsive desire for acceptance and approval. From what I had been told, his maneuvers were usually self-defeating.

After a few games, I was called away and left our visitor to fend for himself. I returned shortly to find him stretched out on the floor in a "trance" with a crowd gathered about him. I was told that he was demonstrating his announced powers of the occult. After a few moments he "awakened," jumped to his feet, and made a "world-shaking prediction." His audience laughed, but their side remarks about a "clod" and "clown" conveyed their irritation.

During the forum period the group worked with a passage of Scripture, trying to discover the historical and personal meanings of the text. Richard stayed right in the thick of the discussion, slashing away with an iconoclastic tongue. Everyone left the meeting disgusted, angry with him and probably also with me—I had been expected to put this egotistical "atheist" in his place with a few well-chosen anathemas. My apparent permissiveness, however, paid off. Richard remained to talk, and at the end accepted an invitation to visit me in my study.

Some time after Richard and I had begun a schedule of dialogue, I learned that his father had been hospitalized. I visited him in his room and listened to a pathetic story of vocational frustration—job discrimination and economic injustice. This man saw himself the victim of management's failure to appreciate talent. Following his release, I called to ask if I might visit the family at home. When I arrived I was greeted warmly, told where to sit, and then introduced to the children and their mother—who were also told where to sit. Conversation was largely confined to father and me, despite my efforts to involve the family. Again I observed an angry, dominant, and manipulative parent. I began to make connection between this controlling authority figure and Richard's angry rejection of a Father-God during our theological discussions.

A simplistic interpretation, in terms suggested by the psychiatrist Thomas Harris, would likely see Richard as the kind of person whose behavior communicates to his world, "I'm OK—You're not OK."* Having failed to experience affirming love from his parents, a frustrated father and submissive mother, he had been obliged to resort to his own "stroking." Now in middle adolescence, with aggressive use of his intellectual powers he was compulsively putting down all those whom he perceived as nonstrokers. His strange acting-out striving for love and acceptance had made him a tragic figure.

It was not for some weeks, until Richard had tested my patience and listening acceptance, that he could relax during our counseling sessions and tolerate two-way communication. It was difficult to break through his defenses. Indeed, there were occasions, I must confess, when I became defensive. Especially under such trying circumstances, one has to be reminded of the conditions which counseling must presumably meet if it is to be therapeutically effective.

Effective Counseling

From his long experience as psychotherapist, Carl Rogers identifies three basic characteristics of the successful counselor: congruence, empathy, and unconditional positive regard.* By congruence he means being one's genuine self without pretense or façade, aware of one's feelings and able to communicate them when appropriate, and emotionally free to meet the counselee in an open person-to-person relationship; the counselor must be "transparently real." To be empathic is to be able to enter sensitively into the private world of the counselee with reasonably accurate understanding and to be able to interpret and communicate the essentials of that understanding; it is to get at the other's personal meanings without becoming involved with one's own uncertainties, fears, and angers. The counselor needs this ability if he is to begin to describe and make clear what the other's inner world is really like, and help the counselee respond with insight. Rogers's third characteristic, unconditional positive regard, means to accept the person totally and nonjudgmentally; the relationship must be one of "outgoing positive feeling without reservation and without evaluations." It is when the counselee experiences this quality of affirmation that he or she is freed to abandon constrictive behavior patterns, and this is necessary before growth can begin.

Effective counseling makes heavy demands upon a leader. It requires a healthy self-acceptance and self-understanding. For me, the time came when I recognized the importance of securing counseling for myself; I needed to work through some of my emotional blind spots so that I might become a more effective pastor and counselor. In working with Richard I realized the importance of the counselor's own emotional condition and self-esteem.

An avid reader, Richard eagerly accepted my library recommendations. Rollo May's *Man's Search for Himself* is a book I have loaned to many an older youth eager to explore the psychology of creative selfhood.* A less sophisticated young person than Richard might be given such a book as John Powell's paperback, *Why Am I Afraid to Tell You Who I Am?*† Richard devoured everything I offered and reveled in his new knowledge.

Gaining Insight

Knowledge *about* self, however, is not equivalent to self-knowledge, or better, self-understanding. For weeks Richard did not see himself as a person with problems. Richard seemed to think of our conversations as a mutual exploration of intriguing ideas—theological and psychological. I was his mentor, not his counselor. It was not until I was reasonably certain that our trust relation could tolerate confrontation that I began to face him with his offensive ways with people. Gradually, he allowed himself to feel the hurt inside and to accept himself as a young person in trouble.

As his reading became personally relevant Richard began to talk about his relationships with his father and with peers. He began to work his way through, at least intellectually, to an understanding of his conflict with his father, though his only resolution of that conflict was to keep his distance. His preoccupation was more with peer relationships. He was especially eager for the companionship of girls. One day he acknowledged that girls refused his invitations to date. We looked at various possible reasons. I recall this as one of the more painful sessions. With growing awareness of his problem, he nevertheless sought to protect himself with such remarks as "Well, I can't dance." At some risk, I seized upon the remark with the thought in mind of trying to create a situation that might help him improve his peer relationships.

In my pastorates I had always cultivated professional relationship with persons in the community whose services could contribute to the church's ministries—men and women in education, psychiatry, medicine, social work, and the YMCA and YWCA, some of whom were members of my congregation. In Richard's case, I had more than one visit with his high school adviser, and in this instance sought the help of the teacher of the performing arts. She agreed to have Richard join a beginners' dancing class. After some hesitation, Richard decided to "give it a try." He also accepted my suggestion that he consult with a dermatologist.

After some weeks of solo learning in the dancing class, the members were invited to choose a partner for the real thing. However incredible this account may appear, the fact is that when Richard approached the girl of his choice and was about to take her hand, he paled and slumped to the floor in a faint. At our next counseling session, he painfully confessed that he had "blown it." During that visit Richard cried.

Making Choices

A counselor functioning from an existentialist perspective will often say in effect to a counselee, "Be!" It is a psychotherapeutic conviction that not until the suffering person is emotionally free to *be* the suffering self, i.e., to feel and acknowledge the hurt, is change likely to occur. Richard had first to say at an authentic emotional level of being "I'm Not OK" before the new and healthier self could emerge. According to Rollo May, however, the belief that when one gets enough insight he or she will make the right growth decision is but a half-truth; the other half is that the counselee will never be able to see the truth until he or she is ready for decision about one's life.* It was the dance fiasco that brought Richard to a decision about life. He really wanted to be a person who could dance, that is, to be socially acceptable and to experience the pleasure of peer participation. He began to make choices.

It was soon thereafter that Richard accepted an invitation to attend a Summer Assembly for youth at which I was to be an instructor. We went together. There, as an unknown in a friendly environment, Richard had opportunity to make a fresh start. I remember especially his venture into sports. As center fielder on a baseball team, he played so deep that every ball hit his way would roll some distance before he could lay a glove on it. But Richard had such a hefty arm that he could throw the ball all the way to home plate, however distant—and on every play he pegged it there whether a runner was headed for home or not! Richard's team effort was accepted in good spirit, however. That was typical of the two weeks—a friendly and affirming acceptance that gave him a new sense of self-identity, a good feeling of "me-ness."

Richard continued to see me for counseling over the period of a year. During this time there remained continuing evidence of insecurity about his peer associations and unhappiness with his home life, but as Richard was now more in touch with his inner self and its motives, he also became less aggressive and more self-affirming. Emotionally he was beginning to say "I'm OK—You're OK."* He knew and I knew that he was going to "make it."

Changing Behavior

Not all counseling relationships with youth are sustained as long as that with Richard. Roger was what Harris would call an "I'm Not OK—You're OK" youth of seventeen years. Tall and awkward in his movements, he tried always to remain in the background of the youth activities. He had come from Canada during the year and had been with us but a few months. During an afternoon of recreation, I got next to Roger and during the conversation invited him to stop by my office. A week later he appeared.

Like Richard that first day, Roger paced the floor. Finally, offering little more than a mumbled excuse, he left. He returned again a week later. This time I said to him, "Roger, it's probably very painful for you to say what's on your mind, but I'm ready to listen if you want to talk." Again pacing the floor and with hands shaking he hesitantly began his story of unhappy childhood, divorced parents, and the present unsatisfactory living conditions with his mother and stepfather. I considered this a good beginning and expected continuing progress in our counseling relationship. But week after week, Roger covered the same ground of unhappiness. There was only one item added to his story: he felt he was not good enough for the youth fellowship, and threatened to leave.

How do we help a troubled person get off emotional dead center? The answer, of course, depends upon one's philosophy and technique of counseling. "Behavior modification" is a counseling approach that focuses not upon insight but on a change of behavior to effect emotional growth. A counselor friend tells of clients whose initial response to therapy is to indulge in endless "psychiatric storytelling." That describes Roger. I heard his story over and over. What could I do to break the circuit?

The approach of the behaviorist counselor is to work to change the pattern of behavior so that the client experiences a good feeling about what he is *doing*. Intuitively, I sought a way of engaging Roger in some activity in which he could enjoy a sense of achievement and self-acceptance. During a visit with Roger's high school adviser, I learned that he had an inventive mind and was then experimenting with an electronic device of his own invention. I found Roger in the electric shop working with what he called his "gadget." As he showed me what it could do, I had an inspiration. Occasionally on a Sunday night, our recreation period during youth fellowship would feature our own young people with talent in music or some other field. With my fingers crossed, I said, "Roger, I want you to bring that gadget of yours to Sunday's meeting and give the group a demonstration." At first he felt threatened by the thought of being featured before his peers, but he was finally persuaded to perform.

The persuasion paid off. Beyond my fondest dreams for Roger, he "did his thing" with poise and group approval. It was a persoanl triumph. More than that, a miracle! From that night Roger began to blossom. He had a delightful sense of humor and could tell a story with a British accent most effectively. With the beginning of the following year, his manifest competence as a leader and his evident acceptance by the group won him the presidency of the youth fellowship. By means of these encounters, and the affirming confidence communicated by the church's adult leadership, Roger was enabled to reestablish a *sense of basic trust* in his peer group and in himself. He could now say, "You're OK and I'm OK."

Facing Guilt

The pain of guilt feelings is often too severe to share in a direct personal encounter even when help is desperately desired. One morning I opened a letter from Judy, a junior college girl, which concluded with the request, "Either condemn me or forgive me!" She had been a member of our youth fellowship for some months, a quiet but intent participant in our discussion of religion and human relations. A week before writing, she had stayed behind to speak to me but after a halting effort said that she would prefer talking another time.

In the thirteen-page letter she told of her distress. After some weeks of dating, she had accepted her friend's urging to live with him. Within a few months the relationship faltered and she left. At first she was hurt and angry: she had been "used" sexually. This reaction was followed by feelings of guilt and remorse. She became increasingly depressed and unable to sleep or study. Finally at the risk of condemnation and rejection, she wrote the letter. Her participation in the life of the church had given her the courage of confession.

On reading the letter I immediately called Judy by phone and invited her to come to my study. I could have rationalized the experience to assure her that morality is relative to cultural climate, that the climate was changing. I could have characterized the affair as a growing-up experiment and maturing experience. Judy's need, however, was forgiveness. There were tears and talk. The talk was not probing but a sharing of the meaning of relationships—the love and affection she had been seeking. At the end we sat for some moments in silence, then prayed together a prayer of forgiveness and request for a new beginning.

Judy expressed a desire to find a more active place in the life of the church. She was not emotionally ready to teach a church school class but agreed to assist in developing a study–worship unit for the junior-highs. This she could do "behind the scenes" and in the more secure relationship with me. Our major resource was a romanticized story of Jesus' boyhood and youth. Each with a copy, we would read a chapter and together decide upon the features to be presented in story and pictorial forms. An art student, Judy did a series of pastel panels of Jesus and his young friends which she arranged each Sunday as the focus of the worship center. The delight of the junior-highs, in response especially to the art work, made our effort at creative curriculum designing worthwhile in its own right. Its additional value was the opportunity it afforded for relationship and counseling.

The Importance of Relationship

Counseling can often be important in helping youth discover their own growth resources. One evening, during the worship portion of the youth meeting, I noted a high soprano voice singing a descant to a familiar hymn arrangement. The voice belonged to Marian, one of two sisters, both in their mid-teens, whose mother had died during their infancy. The paternal grandmother had assumed the responsibility of their rearing. Marian, the elder sister, was a quiet, shy person, not quite sure of herself in social situations. It was at Grandmother's insistence that she had come to the meeting that night. She had remained inconspicuous through the early activities, but now, as a lover of music, was participating in the worship with obvious pleasure. At the close of the service I spoke to her and congratulated her on her lovely voice. Some time later, I asked Marian if she might be interested in studying voice. She was pleased with the idea but was not sure that Grandmother would be. My next move was to make Grandmother's acquaintance and to talk things over. In the end Marian studied with a fine teacher, took her place in the church choir, and with a new sense of accomplishment and self-esteem became a less dependent and socially freer person.

Some youth, especially the seriously troubled ones, find it difficult to enter into a counseling relationship. They are reluctant to reveal their discomfort, thinking that to do so is to admit to being a "square." Or at best they are ambivalent as they conjure up threatening images of encounter with the "shrink." Unfortunately, if the pastoring leader assumes that "they will come when they really need it," many young people—even many faithful churchgoers—will probably go without sorely needed help. Dropping out, running away, abuse of drugs and alcohol—all dramatize the desperate desire of some youth to escape from the sense of lostness and alienation experienced by so many. Against this background of contemporary stress and strain, the church is obliged to see its counseling service to youth as an aspect of its evangelical mission. I am not advocating any dramatic effort to gather in the troubled—or probe for problems—but simply that leaders be in continuing touch and conversation with their youth, and discerning of need if and when it arises. Youth respond more readily to offers of help where there is a prior relationship of warmth, acceptance, and understanding. Relationship, as we have seen from the outset, is the key to personal ministry.

Improving Skills

Rapport needs to be established, but then also maintained. That done, however, the task is only just begun. The counseling leader must proceed with insight and skill, for counseling is a continuing process involving untiring care. Quite apart from any crisis, the pastoral counselor needs to be asking the kinds of questions that can be helpful in furthering the therapeutic dialogue:

What is going on in this youth's inner world, the world of private meanings?

What are the factors, particularly the relationships, which are functioning in this person's situation?

In what way is the family involved?

What attitudes toward himself or herself do I pick up, not only from the spoken word but from "body language" as well?

What feelings do I detect? How is this youth feeling about himself or herself? How is this person feeling in the encounter with me?

Where is this person on the life pilgrimage? How is it going? What movement do I see? What direction?

What creative resources does this youth have which will maximize the potential for change and growth?

What possible specific thing or things might be done now that will help to alleviate present or future distress, solve a problem, or promote self-affirmation and self-acceptance?

And that first and foremost question: What do I say and do that will help to open up the conversation?

Learning to ask these questions and to discern the variety and levels of answers comes from training and experience. Among these learnings, it is important to add, is an awareness of when to consult and when to refer. It is crucially important to discern the depth at which this youth's problem lies and to sense when professional psychotherapeutic help is called for. A church should make available to its leaders resource persons to whom they can turn for advice and guidance, especially in this field of counseling.

Seminary graduates usually have had some kind of clinical training. Lay leaders of youth often have not, though some may occasionally be fully-trained psychologists or members of one or another of the helping vocations. Whatever their background, adult leaders of youth should be encouraged to read further and to participate in encounter groups, communications workshops, and sensitivity training labs to improve their own skills. Youth deserve the best of skilled leadership.

At a recent meeting of parents and youth leaders, in which the discussion centered on the importance of relationship, a mother said with feeling at one point, "Yes, but I also want my young people to have the kind of leader who can help them develop a Christian faith." She was calling for a competence that is not only alert to the need for self-identity and growth but that aids youth in building a structure of meaning and value in the context of their biblical-theological heritage. This is the point where journey and pilgrimage merge in the life of maturing adolescents.

6. Shaping a Vision of Life

Beverly is a composer of religious ballads. A teen-ager, she provides her own guitar accompaniment as she sings to herself and occasionally before her church friends. One of her ballads is entitled "he's just a friend, but mine":*

sometimes when things don't go right
i kneel by my bed and pray to a God I know.
when trouble comes
and you're right in the middle
pray to him, he listens.
when temptation strikes
like a kind with no mercy,
God really cares, just ask him.
when ya need a friend
with love and understanding,
you're talking about my lord jesus.
here's freedom
which only love can express.
he's my jesus, he's my lord.
sometimes when things are going great,
i kneel by my bedside and give thanks to the God above.
ladybugs,
butterflies,
happy things and my lord jesus.

With these words Beverly has given religious interpretation to the typical happenings and moods of growing up. It is her way of articulating a faith to live by as a young, experimenting Christian.

Religion in Adolescence

Not until middle adulthood, Erikson tells us, is an ideology or mature faith (a vision of life) possible. The beginnings, however, are made in childhood and youth. The religion of childhood is simplistic, little more than ideas held as stories about Jesus and God. Faith remains implicit, as an acquired sense of basic trust. With the onset of adolescence, however, religion becomes existentially functional—"for real," as teen-agers say. Characteristic of adolescence are the confrontations with parents and other authority figures, concern about personal appearance, conflict over sexual maturing, the discipline of schooling, decisions of right and wron , a passion for social acceptance, and, for this generation, the lure of alcohol and drugs. These are the pressures which draw youth to religion as a source of solace, forgiveness, and hope. Beverly's ballad is a confession of faith, a statement of personal relationship with an ultimate source of care and counseling—"he's my jesus, he's my lord." Identity formation as pilgrimage provokes for the adolescent not only the question, Who am I? but also the question, Whose am I? and its fulfillment involves I-Thou commitment and devotion.

Not all teen-age religion is comprehended in this reflective teen-ager's verse. There are "varieties of religious experience." Response to religion is conditioned by vulnerability to emotional pressure, and by the behavior patterns and coping strengths one brings to the encounter. Generally speaking, for those whose early crises were happily resolved within the supportive nurture of family and church community, encounter with religion during adolescence is symbolic confirmation and articulation of a faith learned in the years of infancy and childhood as a sense of basic trust. As with Beverly, Jesus Christ becomes the source of one's sense of worth, meaning, and moral guidance, and of one's recovery from guilt and alienation. Such faith may represent conformity to parental belief and practice. However, it may also be an expression of one's newly acquired sense of independence, one's own creative, critical mind-set.

For other youth, encounter with religion "for real" is a highly emotional experience that resolves serious conflict by way of "surrender," a conversion event that radically changes belief, attitude, and life-style. One youth, suddenly appearing home from college, startled his middle-class Protestant professional parents with the greeting, "God bless you! The Lord loves you. I love you. Praise the Lord!" Having sold his "worldly goods," Jay is now living with his "sisters and brothers" of the "Children of God" in the Cave of Jesus somewhere in Mexico. He is ministering to the dispossessed of that nation as well as to wandering hippies from the North. When questioned about his meager material existence, he explained, "None of this stuff everyone thinks so much about matters to me. It doesn't give true happiness. Look at out country, our church and nonchurch people: drugs, alcohol, tranquilizers, misuse of sex, broken families, keeping up with the Joneses, war." Of the results of such ministry, Jay writes, "The fruits are really fabulous."

A similar story, with a slightly different ending, was told me by the father of a teen-age daughter. Moody, irritable, and in constant conflict with her parents—a family of religious commitment and theological sophistication—she began attending the "Jesus People" meetings downtown. In no time, her father reports, she gave every evidence of being an emotionally mature person, apparently secure and self-affirming, able to relate appreciatively to her family, and committed to a socially useful life. Following high school graduation, she spent a year as a social work aide in the mountains of Kentucky, and is now preparing for a career in nursing. She explains the transformation simply by saying that Jesus Christ came into her life. The father adds a significant footnote to the story. He says that once his daughter had worked through her emotional crisis as a member of the "Jesus People," she lost interest in the movement. It is his perception that while grateful for her experience of "saving grace," she could not remain satisfied with the group's simplistic theology. Intellectually she required a more disciplined vision of life.

The Importance of Disciplined Thinking

The neo-Pentecostal movement among today's youth reflects a cultural period when depersonalizing social forces and a new individual freedom—easily misperceived as license—add to the burden of growing up. For many youth caught in the web of cultural confusion, the "Children of God" and the "Jesus People" have given them emotional security and a new way of life. In addition to these theologically radical groups, the evangelical spirit has found organizational expression in such groups as the Crusade for Christ, the Fellowship of Christian Athletes, and Young Life. It is from these and kindred groups, Martin Marty observes, that churches of middle-class America have borrowed or rediscovered "soul."*

Marty, writing of the "spirit" movement in contemporary religion, cautions the churches on the one hand against neglect of "soul," and on the other against the neglect of their interpretive function. He tells of an encounter with a Jesus enthusiast at a recent youth conference who said to him, "Professor, you probably are Christian, but you are too intellectual . . . so complicated. . . ."† Reflecting upon the incident, Marty quotes a colleague who said to him, "It's dangerous to be ignorant. There is going to be a lot of religion around, and an awful lot is going to be harmful to humans unless interpreted." Marty acknowledges that "the overinterpreted life is not living," but he reminds us as well that the "uninterpreted life is not worth living."‡ The church fails its youth if it lacks spirit, but it fails them equally if it does not encourage the discipline of critical thought in shaping a vision of life that can provide intelligent direction.

Youth as individuals vary greatly in their ideological interests. Some are politically active and find here their focus of religious commitment. There is the cult of the apocalyptic with Hal Lindsey's *The Late Great Planet Earth* as the authoritative text.§ Following upon the "Death of God" controversy, many sophisticated older youth resolved the issue by declaring themselves nontheistic Christian humanists. There is a lively interest in the Eastern religions with serious excursions into Zen Buddhism, transcendental meditation, and the practice of yoga.‖ The filming of "The Exorcist" has reinforced a fascination for the occult; all teen-agers know the signs of the zodiac and their meanings for personal fortune. There is also new interest in the Hebrew-Christian Bible, bringing high school people out to early breakfast study or to afternoon and eveing dialogues with Scripture. As youth sense their identity as global persons, they invariably reach toward the interests and resources of a pluralistic and ecumenical world society. Leaders of youth today must necessarily be discerning of cultural trends and flexible in guiding the intellectual-theological explorations of the young. The danger, as Margaret Mead has expressed it, is a "mishmash religion." Leaders should take seriously the cautions of Marty and Mead, and with disciplined use of Scripture enable youth to ground a fresh vision of life in their own biblical heritage at the risk of erratic and superficial explorations.

One group of youth, the kind of attractive young people with whom one enjoys working, confessed that they did not like to discuss what Christians are "supposed" to be like. "We want to be Christian in our own way." I was impressed by their openness and honesty, their apparent lack of racial-ethnic prejudice, their ethical sensitivity and service-mindedness. They acknowledged their church commitment. If I understand their protest, it was against having to engage in critical theological reflection. How can we learn to motivate and engage youth in serious thought and discussion, in what the eighteenth-century theologian Kierkegaard called "existential thinking"? For him existential thinking is intentional and passionate—thinking that "cares terribly about the truth it seeks, for on the outcome hinges the whole meaning and significance of life."* How do we help our youth to become disciplined in existential thinking?

The Bible and Youth

Two young ministers of my acquaintance have acquired commendable skill at this kind of leadership. Dwight and Stan are theologically knowledgeable, understanding of youth, and discussion-oriented in their teaching method. They differ in their curricular approach. Dwight begins with the biblical-historical, Stan with the contemporary interests and concerns of youth. Their respective approaches, both educationally sound, are instructive.

A Biblical–Historical Approach

One Sunday morning Dwight made a few explanatory remarks to his church school class, then distributed copies of a mimeographed statement containing Scripture, questions, and instructions for use. The caption, "How Jesus Handled This Situation" was followed by the text of Mark 1:12-13: "The Spirit immediately drove him into the wilderness. And he was in the wilderness forty days, tempted by Satan; and he was with the wild beasts; and the angels ministered to him." Parallel accounts from Matt. 4:1-11 and Luke 4:1-13 were also included.

Then came the questions: These passages are referred to as the Temptation of Jesus. What do you make of the story? How is Jesus tempted? Putting it in your own words, what do you think the temptations were? How did Jesus handle this crisis situation?

In addition, Dwight asked: What significance do you see in these passages for your life? What are some of the temptations you face, and how do you handle these situations?

The class arranged itself in several groups to work with their assignment. When the groups had reassembled Dwight received their reports, continued the discussion, and added comment. The list of current temptations included: overeating, refusing to study, cutting classes, cheating on tests, dropping out of school, losing one's temper and blowing up, expressing prejudice, engaging in sex relations, breaking the law, refusing to study, copping out, and taking one's life. Both humorous and sobering comments were made as the list was reviewed. Limited confessions were made. There was pensive silence while the teacher called attention to the frequent listing of copping out and suicide. He spoke of the increasing mood of despair among youth. Dwight regards the list as diagnostic data for individual counseling and as theme content for subsequent instruction.

The use of Scripture that morning confronted the class with

their own existential situation. In the intimacy of the small sharing group they were free to identify and to examine—even if only superficially at first—their values and life-styles. The existential thinking of such a class session is continuous with the growth group experience. The feature of the instructional approach is the role of the leader as biblical exegete and theological commentator who contributes out of his or her research and study. During an extended study unit youth engage in research themselves with the use of commentaries, dictionaries, and other resources.

Dwight will continue to develop teaching-learning units for the purpose of furthering self-understanding in the light of Christian meanings and values. He hopes in this connection to apply the techniques of the current "values clarification" movement in education. The method is to assist youth in becoming aware of the beliefs and values they prize and are willing to stand up for both in and out of class. The teacher uses materials and techniques which affirm and aid the student in considering alternative modes of thinking, feeling, and acting. Through the use of case studies, multiple-choice exercises, role playing, storytelling, and creative writing youth are taught to weigh the pros and cons of alternative behaviors against the probable consequences of their decision. They are helped to reflect upon whether their actions correspond with their stated beliefs and, if not, how to bring the two into closer harmony. Teaching of this kind is pragmatic in that students are given options to test both in and out of class. The practical procedures offered by Simon, Howe, and Kirschenbaum are especially appropriate for use in the church school and youth fellowship program as a supplement to Bible study and theological reflection.*

A Contemporary-Concerns Approach

Stan's teaching approach is different from that of Dwight. Stan has penetrated deeply into the thought world of modern youth and feels that he is most successful in his use of Scripture when he begins with the interests and concerns of the youth themselves. He finds, for example, in the songs of Cat Stevens contrasting existential themes: light (truth) vs. darkness (falsehood), searcher vs. answer-man, authenticity vs. phoniness, journey (life) vs. stasis (death). Youth, he observes, listen not only to the beat but also to the message.

One evening Stan's young people listened to the folk song "On the Road to Find Out." The ballad tells the adventures of a young man who leaves his "happy home" to clear out his mind and to learn what life is about. It is a modern myth of today's hero journey. Indeed, it becomes a pilgrimage inasmuch as the search is for truth. The young man walks with feelings of ambivalence. He looks back upon his past with nostalgia, having left family and friends, but finds that he is "locked toward the future" and must go on. With guitar accompaniment, Stevens sings the existentialist's theme of the authentic life that is learned and earned by dint of courageous encounter. Listening to the recording, youth easily identify with the traveler and readily talk of their own rough road "to find out."

Toward the end of the song, the "hero" learns that it is of value to him to "pick up a good book" along the way. One can learn of truth from others, from the written word. That night, as integral to their discussion of journey/pilgrimage, Stan asked the group to work with him in discerning relevant meanings in the Gospel of John. Thus they talked about light and darkness, life and death, honesty and deceit—all within the context of their own growing-up "rough road." Stan reported that his young people became deeply involved as he helped them to find personal meaning in these themes and their relationship to the One who had been sent that they might find life and find it "more abundantly."

Pilgrimage in the Bible

Stan and Dwight have both found a wealth of teaching resources to give biblical perspective to pilgrimage—Abraham's going forth on faith alone, Jacob's flight from acts of deceit, Moses' march to freedom, Jonah's reluctant mission to Nineveh, Jesus' setting his face steadfastly toward Jerusalem, and that remarkable happening on the road to Damascus.

Parables, too, have to do with journeys. Youth respond with insight to the parable of the prodigal son. They identify with the younger son who sought freedom from home in a world of excitement. By means of role playing and fantasy, they see ᵗhemselves in precisely those predicaments which brought the young man to the depths of despair. They speculate about hope for themselves in the event of "coming to himself." Like the Pharisees who first heard the story, they find the "old man" an incredibly loving figure. "Can this part of the story be really true?" they ask. They have no problem recognizing the elder brother and acknowledge the self-understanding the whole story brings to their sibling relationships.

The parable of the good Samaritan is also about a journey—from Jerusalem to Jericho. Youth enjoy "working over" the priest and Levite and their contemporary counterparts—good members of the religious establishment. They find a "shocker" in the story, however, when it is pointed out that "we all" pass by on the other side. Discussion then turns to one's own attitudes and behavior: self-righteousness, insensitivity, uninvolvement, hypocrisy, prejudice, and irresponsibility. Their idealism is kindled when talk focuses upon the compassion and magnanimity of the road-traveling Samaritan and the trust of the innkeeper, but skepticism is also expressed as they wonder where such persons, especially among themselves, are to be found today. Youth never fail to face themselves honestly in an atmosphere of freedom and acceptance.

A favorite Genesis journey for youth is that of Jacob. A group worked with the crisis that occurred in Jacob's life at the Jabbok. After recounting his life story and placing it in the context of Israel's history, I engaged some young people in a personal appropriation of the crisis experience. They took hold especially when I asked them to reflect upon the significance of a name and their name in particular:

What's in a name? Does it tell something about a person? Do you think of your name as an important part of your identity?

Do you know why your parents gave you your name? How do you feel about your name? What are you called by your friends? How do you feel about that word? Do you ever wish for another name? Why? What other name would you choose? Why? How does one give significance to a name? Does it have something to do with character?

For these young people such questioning brought to the surface concerns about themselves—how they perceive and appraise themselves, how they communicate an image to others, how they are perceived and received by peers and adults, and what it means to bear the name of Christian.

Fitting the "Little Story" into the "Big Story"

Theology is currently much interested in the "storytelling" approach to its task of shaping a vision of life. Youth leaders can use the approach to good effect. To engage in telling one's "little story" can be helpful in fitting it into the "big story." This enables a person to see his or her existence with an enhanced measure of coherent. historical meaning.

"On the Road to Find Out" is but one of many themes readily available in youth's ideological world in terms of which they may tell their "little story" and relate it to their religious heritage. When leaders are aware of the Bible's power to illumine contemporary human existence, the world of the Bible which is so often strange to youth need not remain so. Leadership needs on the one hand to be discerning of what in youth's experience "turns them on"—its storytelling potential—and on the other to acquire the teaching skill of biblical hermeneutics.

Hermeneutic simply means the task of interpretation, of determining what a passage *meant* historically and what it *means* presently. Biblical hermeneutics attempts to translate the word of an ancient religious culture into its contemporary equivalent. Methodologically, to do hermeneutics means to become engaged with Scripture dialogically. It means listening to the words of the text as Word, asking questions of the text, thinking both historically and existentially, and talking over with fellow searchers the emerging message until one's life is confronted and illumined. Interpretation of the Bible is not an academic exercise of learning what the text is saying in general, but a personal confrontation with what is being said in particular. The address is to the one who engages the text. We have long thought—and said—that "I" interpret the text. However, I inevitably approach Scripture subjectively, i.e., I always bring to it my presuppositions about the Bible and about life, and hence interpret it with personal bias. When, on the other hand, I begin to engage the text openly and honestly and with the aid of scholarship, I find the text interpreting *me.* I begin to say, "Yes, that describes me." This is precisely the experience intended by the hermeneutic-dialogic method, which seeks to illumine my self-understanding from a fresh theological perspective and to confront me with a decision for or against the authentic existence which the Bible offers.

The dialogic or discussion method of Bible study lends itself to hermeneutic purpose, i.e., to the appropriation of personal meaning. The role of the leader is essentially twofold: to facilitate dialogue and to make available the findings of scholarship. The following procedural guidelines are suggested for use with numbers large enough to work as small group study teams:

1. Create a climate of community; arrange persons in groups of five or six and, if need be, suggest techniques for getting acquainted.

2. Instruct members to read the passage reflectively as though in dialogue with the writer—inquiring, feeling along with, talking back to, but not fighting or trying to correct; one is free to disagree with the writer, but the first task is to try to understand what he is saying.

3. Encourage discussion at the deepest possible level, listening and learning by sharing, exchanging ideas rather than debating, expressing honest feelings; an outline of questions submitted by the leader may serve the process.

4. Introduce the data of biblical research; method may include mini-lecture, mimeographed material, and group use of commentaries, dictionaries, and other helps.

5. Encourage groups to move from what the passage *meant* to what it *means,* with focus upon here-and-now experience.

6. Make oneself available on request as a resource person but not as a final "answer-man."

7. Receive feedback on the small groups' hermeneutic efforts, add commentary, and lead the total group in continued dialogue.

8. Summarize the session.

While the discussion method may be adapted to one's personal leadership style, it does expect an affirmation of group members in the integrity of their participation as lay theologians. Youth need to be accepted at the level of their interpretative competence even as they are nurtured in the acceptance and use of scholarship. Can it ever be a communication of the "good news" of Christ's love for persons to *impose* a position, however exegetically correct? Youth are open to exploration and will accept confrontation when "truth" is made optional rather than arbitrary. One proceeds with maturity of patience and skill to facilitate a learning process in which participants are motivated to search for themselves and to grow.

Variety in Activities and Resources

Conditions for creative Bible study of this kind are met when the hermeneutic process is furthered by the use of selected activity techniques. One group found it an illuminating experience during their Palm Sunday study unit to fantasize the roles of those participating in that historic event—Jesus, the disciples, members of the welcoming crowd, temple officials, even the donkey, palm trees, cobblestones, and strewn garments. In a role play of the prodigal son for youth leaders, a high school coach who thought of himself as a tough disciplinarian, was deeply moved by his experience as the compassionate father. At a weekend retreat youth simulated the fourth-century Council of Nicea. The competing ecclesiastical factions used the popular cinquain poetry form to compose and present their theological positions for debate, with a committee of "bishops" writing the final statement of faith. Such "reality learning" experiences fruitfully supplement the discipline of exegesis.

The communicative arts contribute equally to creative learning. One usually thinks of the film, recordings, video tape, and television as the important media in this category. Reproductions of the master painters and such classic photography as Edward Steichen's superb collection in the *Family of Man* are also of educational value.* Using a painting (or a photograph) such as Picasso's "Guernica," two questions are put to the study group: What do you see happening here? and, Where do you see it happening in your life? Paul Tillich regards great art as an unsurpassed means of confronting persons with the issues of life and evoking the courage and power to face the human predicament. This too is hermeneutic.

The use of art implies that shaping a vision of life can be furthered when the process is literally made visual. The picturing of one's life story with paint or pastel can serve the same objective. Discussing some aspect of their pilgrimage, youth may be asked to project onto a sheet of newsprint some personal experience, possibly a turning point in their life. They may do a line drawing or an abstract of the event. Once they have pictured the self, sometimes working in as well the major events of their entire life-story, they are normally eager to share it with their peers. An abstract of the experience, which is usually preferred, is especially effective for the purpose of interpreting the self-in-situation. This use of expressive art may be an extension of dialogue with Scripture or the occasion to introduce the group to relevant biblical-historical material—fitting one's "little story" into the "big story." Frequently one or more persons will ask for time to talk further of the insights which occurred during the exercise.

There is an abundance of such techniques available to leaders from both denominational and independent publishing sources. When faithfully used as hermeneutical tools to interpret the relevance of the great religious and ethical themes of the church's tradition and present mission, they have the power to draw youth into learning that charts their pilgrim journey and to reinforce them in their commitment.

Hermeneutics and "History-Making"

Finally, if hermeneutics is to shape a vision of life that is fully biblical it must motivate the full investment of a socially responsible self. The Brazilian religious leader and educator, Paulo Freire, insists that the "word" requires a balance of its two constituent elements: reflection and action. Talk without action is mere verbalism; action without reflection converts the "word" into activism.* Existential thinking, thinking that cares terribly about the truth it seeks, fulfills its purpose when it engages persons in what Ross Snyder calls "history-making."†

In a Lenten issue of "The Reflector," a newsletter written and published by a church youth group, announcement was made that during Holy Week the group would caravan to a Mexican village to assist church members there in repairing their building and to direct a program for their children. Another church group volunteered to canvass their local community in the interest of political reform. Clif left college for a year to organize Zero-Population study-action groups in his hometown. This is history-making.

A teen-age member of a local Council for Peace remarked that her participation in its program of education and action had given significance to her life: "I feel I count for something." One is reminded of Justice Holmes's observation that we participate "in the passion and action of our time at the peril of otherwise being judged not having lived."‡

In a time of growing cynicism and apathy, youth must be helped experientially to understand the prophetic side of the Christian faith. Faith is a passion for social justice as well as an experience of Personal Presence. The Epistle of James declares that "faith without works is dead."

In the thought of Erik Erikson youth without ideology are youth without identity, and their life is lived in a state of confusion and alienation. It is a major goal of personal ministry that youth shall have a vision of life that gives integrity, meaning, and social usefulness to their existence.

7. The Call Forward

The rationale, purposes, and procedures of personal ministry need to be seen in a theoretical context that appropriates the data of both psychology and theology. The adolescent experience is both a journey *and* a pilgrimage.

As a clinical observer of behavior, Erik Erikson understands normal human existence as a process of development, through a succession of stages, toward an ever-maturing quality of selfhood. During the years of adolescence, growth is peculiarly motivated by the attraction of identity, i.e., knowing who one is and the meaning of that personal existence. From the perspective of the behavioral sciences, the process of human growth is described as a biological thrust of the organism and a response to psychosocial crises. While stating his position in the classical idiom of psychodynamic theory, however, Erikson admits that he cannot account for this movement toward qualitative life in more adequate terms than those of the biblical explanation that humankind is created in the divine image—a "counterplayer" of God's identity.

In turn, today's theologian grants the biological foundation of growth and the psychosocial processes which affect it, but is committed also to an interpretation of its motivation that assumes an ultimate and transcendent source. In the words of John B. Cobb, Jr., growth toward self-fulfillment is a life of faith lived in response to the "call forward."* According to Cobb's New Testament understanding of divine action, God is present in human processes and events as creative potential, and at the conscious level of experience as a vision luring us with new and richer possibilities for our existence, or, as Jesus said, a "more abundant life." For Cobb the divine "call forward" is "toward intensified life, heightened consciousness, expanded freedom, more sensitive love. . . ." Such experience liberates the self from the "limits and burdens of the past" and makes it possible to find a fulfillment that is personally satisfying and an enrichment of the life of others. "But the way," he adds, "lies through the valley of the shadow of death."* Cobb is describing Christian pilgrimage—the self-conscious, committed, sometimes painfully disciplined striving toward the realization of ideal possibilities envisioned in Christ's coming kingdom of God.

Recalling the hero myths, I am reminded that despite trial and tribulation the hero inevitably triumphs. In the world of reality, however, and certainly in a period of socio-cultural revolution with its confusing impact upon persons, the outcome of youth's journey is not so assured. *Dropping out* and *copping out* are terms permanently fixed in a vocabulary describing what it is like to grow up in the late years of the twentieth century. Some youth "make it," others are obliged to "fake it."

Entering upon the hero journey/pilgrimage and learning to "make it" is conditioned upon a favorable hearing of the "call." As we have seen, the disciplines of democratic process, group and individual guidance, and the use of biblical-historical hermeneutics are essentials of leadership procedure. Important as the facilitative skills remain, however, I am persuaded that it is the personal qualities of leadership which make it possible for youth to hear the "call." Youth need Adult Guarantors, women and men who become an *affirming presence* to youth, whose authentic and open selfhood communicates empathic understanding, unconditional positive regard, and trustworthiness. In response to this maturity of leadership, youth give themselves enthusiastically to the task of cooperatively creating a culture of covenant–caring community and shaping a vision of life. It is in this socio-religious climate, experiencing a relationship of care and counseling, that they are enabled to hear and respond to the "call forward."

Notes

Page

iv. *Martin Buber, *I and Thou,* trans. Ronald Gregor Smith, 2d ed. (New York: Scribner's Sons, 1958), p. 11.

xiii. *Merton P. Strommen, *Profiles of Church Youth* (St. Louis: Concordia, 1963), p. 238.

2. *Erik H. Erikson, *Young Man Luther* (New York: W. W. Norton & Co., 1958), pp. 17, 37, 147, 156.

3. *Ross Snyder, "The Ministry of Meaning" in *Risk* (Geneva, Switzerland: Youth Department of the World Council of Churches and World Council of Christian Education), 1 (1965): 137–143.

4. *Helpful case studies can be found in such books as Evelyn Mills Duvall, *Today's Teen-Agers* (New York: Association Press, 1966); Shirley A. Hamrin and Blanche B. Paulsen, *Counseling Adolescents* (Chicago: Science Research Associates, 1950); Rudolph W. Wittenberg, *On Call for Youth* (New York: Association Press, 1955) and *The Troubled Generation* (New York: Association Press, 1967).

7. *Erikson, *Identity: Youth and Crisis.*

8. *Werner Wolff, *The Personality of the Preschool Child* (New York: Grune & Stratton, 1946), p. xiv.

8. †Henry James, ed., *The Letters of William James* (Boston: Atlantic Monthly Press, 1920), 1:199; quoted in Erikson, *Identity: Youth and Crisis,* p. 19.

19. *Lewis S. Sherrill, *The Struggle of the Soul* (New York: Macmillan Co., 1951).

20. *Ibid., p. 6.

22. *Ross Snyder, *Young People and Their Culture* (Nashville: Abingdon Press, 1969), p. 44.

27. *Thomas Gordon, *Parent Effectiveness Training* (New York: Peter H. Wyden, 1970).

30. *Eric Berne, *Games People Play* (New York: Grove Press, 1964).

34. *Snyder, *Young People and Their Culture,* pp. 160–62.

35. *Reuel L. Howe, *The Miracle of Dialogue* (Greenwich, Conn.: Seabury Press, 1969), p. 9.

Page

35. †Buber, p. 11.

36. *Ibid., p. 75.

36. †Robert C. Ouradnik, "The Middle-Class Quest for Alternatives," *Christian Century*, 3 April, 1974, p. 366.

38. *Carl R. Rogers, *Carl Rogers on Encounter Groups* (New York: Harper & Row, 1970), p. 49.

40. *Harold Bessell and Uvaldo Palomares, *Human Development Program for Institutionalized Teenagers* (San Diego: Human Development Training Institute, 1971), chaps. 1–3.

41. *Rogers, *Encounter Groups*, pp. 4–5.

42. *Thomas C. Oden, *The Intensive Group Experience: The New Pietism* (Philadelphia: Westminster Press, 1973), chaps. 1–2.

43. *Ibid., p. 165.

43. †Donald McNassor, "Identity Counseling for the Older High School Student" (Claremont Graduate School & University Center, Claremont, Calif., 1974).

43. ‡Research Seminar Working Paper, no. 2, "Seeing Through a Glass Darkly: Outer Edges of Identity in the Seventeenth Year of Life" (Claremont Graduate School & University Center, Claremont, Calif., 1960–61), p. 2.

44. *McNassor, pp. 3–5.

48. *Thomas A. Harris, M.D., *I'm OK—You're OK: A Practical Guide to Transactional Analysis* (New York: Harper & Row, 1967), p. 48.

49. *Carl R. Rogers and Barry Stevens, *Person to Person: The Problem of Being Human, A New Trend in Psychology* (Lafayette, Calif.: Real People Press, 1967), pp. 90–96.

50. *Rollo May, *Man's Search for Himself* (New York: W. W. Norton & Co., 1953).

50. †John Powell, S.J., *Why Am I Afraid to Tell You Who I Am?* (Chicago: Peacock Books, Argus Communications, 1969).

51. *Rollo May, Ernest Angel, and Henri F. Ellenberger, eds., *Existence: A New Dimension in Psychiatry and Psychology* (New York: Basic Books, 1958), p. 87.

52. *Harris, p. 43.

58. *Ballad composed by Beverly Waller of Des Moines, Washington; quoted by permission.

61. *Martin E. Marty, *The Fire We Can Light* (Garden City, N. Y.: Doubleday & Co., 1973), p. 110.

61. †Ibid., p. 217.

61. ‡Ibid.

Page

61. §Hal Lindsey and C. C. Carlson, *The Late Great Planet Earth* (Grand Rapids, Mich.: Zondervan, 1970).

61. ‖Tynette Hills and Floyd Ross, *The Great Religions By Which Men Live* (New York: Fawcett Premier Books, 1969).

62. *"That Blessed Word 'Existential,'" editorial in *Christian Century,* 30 November 1955, p. 1392.

64. *Simon, Howe, and Kirschenbaum, *Values Clarification.*

70. *Family of Man* (New York: The Museum of Modern Art, 1955).

71. *Paulo Freire, *Pedagogy of the Oppressed* (New York: Herder & Herder, 1970), pp. 75–76.

71. †Snyder, *Young People and Their Culture,* p. 106.

71. ‡Ibid., p. 110.

72. *John B. Cobb, Jr., *God and the World* (Philadelphia: Westminster Press, 1969), p. 56.

73. *Ibid.

Annotated Bibliography

Blees, Robert. *Counseling With Teen-Agers.* Philadelphia: Fortress Press, 1968. Accounts of growth group experiences and couhseling with youth and their parents by the staff of the First Community Church, Columbus, Ohio.

Blos, Peter. *The Adolescent Personality.* New York: Free Press, 1962. A psychoanalytic study of adolescence, its phases and growing up problems; illustrated from case material.

Clinebell, Howard J., Jr. *Basic Types of Pastoral Counseling.* Nashville: Abingdon Press, 1966. A comprehensive treatment of the varieties of counseling methods based upon a revised model that emphasizes improving relationships and maximizing the counselee's positive personality resources.

———. *The People Dynamic.* New York: Harper & Row, 1972. Strategies for conducting various kinds of groups including growth groups for youth.

De Jong, Arthur J. *Making It To Adulthood.* Philadelphia: Westminster Press, 1972. An Eriksonian interpretation of identity formation and discussion of tasks, moods, feelings, and defenses of adolescent development, with chapters devoted to dating, developing self-esteem, sex ethics, and preparation for marriage.

Dow, Robert Arthur. *Learning Through Encounter.* Valley Forge, Pa.: Judson Press, 1971. The theology and method of nurturing persons through creative human relations in the life of the church.

Erikson, Erik H. *Childhood and Society.* New York: W. W. Norton & Co., 1950. Enlarged ed., 1963. Erikson's first major publication of his interpretation of the "life cycle" and its implications for the rearing of children.

————. *Identity: Youth and Crisis.* New York: W. W. Norton & Co., 1968. An extended treatment of Erikson's "epigenetic principle" with particular reference to the adolescent-youth stage of development.

Ernest, Ken. *Games Students Play.* Milbraie, Calif.: Celestial Arts Publishing Co., 1972. A popular treatment of Eric Berne's transactional analysis with illustrations from "games played" in public school classrooms and how to deal with them creatively.

Fairchild, Roy W. *The Waiting Game.* New York: Thomas Nelson, 1971. One of the "Youth Forum Series," a paperback about youth addressed to youth; a Christian confrontation for those who would "live for the moment."

Gallagher, J. Rowell, M.D., and Harris, Herbert I. *Emotional Problems of Adolescents.* New York: Oxford Press, 1958. The treatment of problems in the areas of achieving independence, sex, anxiety states, homesickness, psychosomatic diseases, scholastic failure, and antisocial behavior.

Hebeisen, Ardyth. *Peer Program for Youth.* Minneapolis: Augsburg Publishing House, 1973. A group interaction plan to develop self-esteem, self-understanding, and communication skills.

Hunter, Archibald M. *The Parables Then and Now.* Philadelphia: Westminster Press, 1971. A popular but scholarly interpretation of Jesus' parables; usable for teaching youth.

Kell, Bill L., and Burow, Josephine M. *Developmental Counseling and Therapy.* Boston: Houghton Mifflin Co., 1970. A personalized account of multiple processes in individual counseling with youth; accent upon interpersonal relations.

Leslie, Robert C. *Sharing Groups in the Church.* Nashville: Abingdon Press, 1971. An account of the place and variety of groups in the life of the church; illustrated from leadership experience.

Little, Sara. *Youth, World and Church.* Richmond, Va.: John Knox Press, 1968. A comprehensive account of a balanced ministry to and with youth; generously illustrated from experimental programs.

MacLennan, Beryce W., and Felsenfeld, Naomi. *Group Counseling and Psychotherapy With Adolescents.* New York: Columbia University Press, 1968. An interpretation of the peer culture and the function of the group as change agent; group leadership and its training; counseling in the areas of boy-girl relations and sex, management of feelings, peer group and the law, relationship to adults and other authority figures, and career choices.

Perrin, Norman. *Rediscovering the Teaching of Jesus.* New York: Harper & Row, 1967. A scholarly work on establishing the authentic teaching of Jesus; an important resource for Bible study.

Raths, Louis Edward; Harmin, Merrill; and Simon, Sidney B. *Values and Teaching.* Columbus, Ohio: Charles E. Merrill Books, 1966. The theory and method of "values clarification" presented and illustrated from classroom practice.

Richards, Lawrence O. *Creative Bible Study.* Grand Rapids, Mich.: Zondervan, 1971. A handbook for small group and individual Bible study with emphasis upon the text's meaning for present existence.

Rood, Wayne R. *On Nurture Christians.* Nashville: Abingdon Press, 1972. A discussion of the educational revolt and the knowledge explosion with implications for nurture in the church.

Scott, Edward M. *The Adolescent Gap.* Springfield, Ill.: Charles C. Thomas, Publishers, 1972. Research findings on drug-using and nondrug-using teens; youth tell their own story.

Simon, Sidney B.; Howe, Leland W.; and Kirschenbaum, Howard. *Values Clarification.* New York: Hart Publishing Co., 1972. A handbook of techniques and exercises for teacher-student use.

Strommen, Merton P. *Five Cries of Youth.* New York: Harper & Row, 1974. An interpretation of adolescence based upon an ecumenical study of church youth.

Wheelis, Allen. *The Quest for Identity.* New York: W. W. Norton & Co., 1958. A psychiatrist's use of narrative to illuminate the theory of identity formation.

Wink, Walter. *The Bible in Human Transformation.* Philadelphia: Fortress Press, 1973. A critique of the historical-critical method of biblical interpretation; proposed sociological and psychoanalytic models of interpretation.